C000108502

The Musical Importance of Being Earnest

A Musical

John Sean O'Mahony and Oscar Wilde

A SAMUEL FRENCH ACTING EDITION

SAMUEL FRENCH

FOUNDED 1830

SAMUELFRENCH-LONDON.CO.UK
SAMUELFRENCH.COM

Copyright © 1988 by Parker Publishing
All Rights Reserved

THE MUSICAL IMPORTANCE OF BEING EARNEST is fully protected under the copyright laws of the British Commonwealth, including Canada, the United States of America, and all other countries of the Copyright Union. All rights, including professional and amateur stage productions, recitation, lecturing, public reading, motion picture, radio broadcasting, television and the rights of translation into foreign languages are strictly reserved.

ISBN 978-0-573-08081-4

www.samuelfrench-london.co.uk

www.samuelfrench.com

FOR AMATEUR PRODUCTION ENQUIRIES

UNITED KINGDOM AND WORLD EXCLUDING NORTH AMERICA
plays@SamuelFrench-London.co.uk
020 7255 4302/01

Each title is subject to availability from Samuel French,

depending upon country of performance.

CAUTION: Professional and amateur producers are hereby warned that THE MUSICAL IMPORTANCE OF BEING EARNEST is subject to a licensing fee. Publication of this play does not imply availability for performance. Both amateurs and professionals considering a production are strongly advised to apply to the appropriate agent before starting rehearsals, advertising, or booking a theatre. A licensing fee must be paid whether the title is presented for charity or gain and whether or not admission is charged.

The professional rights in this play are controlled by Samuel French Ltd, 52 Fitzroy Street, London, W1T 5JR.

No one shall make any changes in this title for the purpose of production. No part of this book may be reproduced, stored in a retrieval system, or transmitted in any form, by any means, now known or yet to be invented, including mechanical, electronic, photocopying, recording, videotaping, or otherwise, without the prior written permission of the publisher. No one shall upload this title, or part of this title, to any social media websites.

The right of John Sean O'Mahony and Oscar Wilde to be identified as author of this work has been asserted by them in accordance with Section 77 of the Copyright, Designs and Patents Act 1988

CHARACTERS

Algernon Moncrieff
John Worthing (Jack)
Mr Lake
1st Shop Assistant
2nd Shop Assistant
Lane, Algernon's manservant
Lady Bracknell
Gwendolen
Miss Prism
Cecily
Dr Chasuble
Merriman, a butler
Ladies and Gentlemen of London, Shop Assistants, Servants, Maids

SYNOPSIS OF SCENES

ACT I

ACT II

MUSICAL NUMBERS

ACT I

1	Overture	Orchestra
2	A Fine and Gracious City	Ladies and Gentlemen of London
2A	Scene change	Orchestra
3	Bunburying	Algernon and Jack
3A	Scene change	Orchestra
4	The Importance of Being Ernest/One Love	Jack and Gwendolen
5	Your Engagement	Lady Bracknell
5A	Your Engagement—continuation	Lady Bracknell and Jack
5B	One Love—underscore	Orchestra
6	Bunburying—reprise	Algernon and Lane
6A	Scene change	Orchestra
7	I Must Write That Down Before I Forget	Cecily and Miss Prism
8	I Need Someone to Rescue Me	Algernon and Cecily
8A	I Must Write That Down—reprise	Cecily
8B	Scene change	Orchestra
9	Every Flower in the Garden	Miss Prism and Dr Chasuble
10	Funeral March	Orchestra
11	The Importance of Being Ernest	Algernon and Cecily
12	Sincerely Yours	Cecily
13	Your Duty as a Gentleman	Jack, Algernon and Servants

ACT II

14	Entr'acte	Orchestra
15	The Importance of Being Ernest	Cecily and Algernon
16	I Am Never Wrong	Gwendolen and Cecily
17	May I Offer You a Cup of Tea?	Cecily and Gwendolen
18	Yes For A Woman We Will	Jack and Algernon
18A	Play-off music	Orchestra
18B	Scene change music	Orchestra
19	One Vital Question	Gwendolen, Cecily, Jack and Algernon
19A	One Love Dance	Orchestra
20	My Ward/Your Engagement	Jack and Lady Bracknell
21	Borne in a Handbag	Miss Prism, Lady Bracknell, Jack and Company
22	One Love/The Importance of Being Ernest	Gwendolen and Company
23	Curtain Calls	
24	Play-out	Orchestra

Music No. 1: Overture

ACT I

SCENE 1

Outside Green Park in the heart of fashionable London

Music No. 2: A Fine and Gracious City

The CURTAIN *opens to reveal a picture made up of members of London society and the people who serve them. After 16 bars of music most exit* L *and* R *leaving only a Flower Girl* UC *and a Messenger*

A Nursemaid enters L *with a pram which she wheels from* L *to* R *and then to the Flower Girl* UC

Three Young Men enter. One walks over to buy a buttonhole from the Flower Girl

The Nursemaid exits

Two Mothers and Daughters enter from opposite sides and greet each other

Mr Lake enters and pauses to buy a buttonhole from the Flower Girl

One Young Man recognizes one of the Daughters. He moves across, doffs his hat and takes her across to introduce his friends. The Mothers remain in deep conversation. The other Daughter moves across to join her friend and the Young Men

A Father and Daughter enter. They greet the Mothers. The Daughter moves across to join the group of young people. The Father goes to buy a buttonhole from the Flower Girl

The Nursemaid enters with her pram and wheels it through the people

The two Mothers and the Father suddenly realize their Daughters have moved away to talk to the Young Men and hurry across to rescue them. All move into position to sing; the two Mothers are LC *and* RC *downstage; behind them are the Daughters and the Flower Girl, with the Nursemaid* UC. *The Gentlemen are slightly upstage either side* L *and* R *as all freeze and look straight out front*

All   This is a fine and gracious city
The very centre of the land
From Hyde Park Gate cross to dear Mayfair
Through Savile Row and right down to the Strand.

Women	This is a fine and lovely city
Mothers	Though some prefer to call it town
Daughters	And some marvellous shops
Men	The very tops
Mothers	And all of them suppliers to the Crown.
Men	This is a fine and wealthy city
	Full of money power and fame
Young Men	And the chance to meet
	If you are discreet
Mothers	But not until we've thoroughly checked your name.
All	This is a fine and gracious city
	With all that's old and grand and new
	But society
Mothers	And propriety
All	Will always govern everything we do.

The group breaks up with the Flower Girl offering flowers to the two Mothers who decline them taking their Daughters off L and R. The Nursemaid wheels her pram off, while the Father leads his Daughter and others off

As the Lights fade US Algernon enters L and moves in a spot to LC DS. He pulls out his fob watch and exits R

Music No. 2A: Scene change

As soon as the shop truck is in position three Shop Assistants enter in step with each other and set the shop table and two chairs LC; two of these exit L and R, one remains at the table sorting swatches of material. Two Shop Assistants enter and place a mirror and hatstand in position RC, then exit into the R alcove of the shop

NB: Throughout the production all scene changes and the movement of props are fully choreographed and undertaken by members of the cast

SCENE 2

Lake's—one of London's most fashionable tailors

The shelves are lined with hats, rolls of cloth, hat boxes etc. There are two dummies, one with a cover on CL and one with a Norfolk jacket R, a movable mirror to the R, a large stick and cane stand DCL, a counter UR, a table L with two chairs. A bow window separates the shop from the scene behind but one can still see anyone passing by outside. There is a changing room to one side

Two Assistants are passing items of clothing to Mr Lake who is fitting John Worthing (Jack) in the changing room

Algernon enters by the C *door*

One Assistant moves from the table to meet him C

1st Assistant Can I help you, sir?

Algernon I'm looking for Mr Ernest Worthing. He had an appointment with Mr Lake this morning at eleven.

1st Assistant Mr Worthing is being fitted by Mr Lake at the moment, sir.

Algernon (*removing his hat*) Kindly tell him that Mr Algernon Moncrieff is here.

Algernon moves towards the cheval mirror R *to inspect his appearance. The Assistant moves to the alcove* R *just as Mr Lake emerges*

1st Assistant There is a Mr Algernon Moncrieff to see Mr Worthing, sir.

Algernon moves to sit in the chair L *of the table, attended by another Assistant who has entered from the* L *alcove*

2nd Assistant (*seeing that Algernon is examining the hats*) Would you like to see some of our latest designs while you're waiting, sir?

Algernon No thank you.

Jack emerges from the alcove wearing a half-finished suit. Mr Lake and other Assistants follow him to his R, *one carrying Jack's normal jacket. Music No. 2 fades. Algernon rises and moves* C *to meet Jack*

Ah, there you are, Ernest.

Jack Good heavens! What are you doing here, Algy?

Algernon As soon as I heard you were back in town I called round to arrange to have dinner with you but your man told me you were here.

Mr Lake When would you like the suit to be delivered, sir?

Jack By Tuesday morning.

Mr Lake Very good, sir. The other jacket will be ready in two minutes.

He helps him off with the half-made jacket and hands it to one of his Assistants who exits L. *He then helps Jack into his normal jacket while another Assistant brings a clothes brush from the table and brushes down Jack's jacket. He then exits into the alcove* R *with the other Assistants*

Algernon Where have you been since last Thursday, Ernest?

Jack Oh, in the country.

Algernon In Shropshire?

Jack (*a bit puzzled*) Shropshire? (*Realizing he's supposed to live there*) Oh Shropshire! Yes, of course.

Algernon What brings you up to town again so quickly?

Jack I must speak to Gwendolen about a very important matter.

Algernon Aunt Augusta won't approve.

Jack May I ask why?

Algernon The way you flirt with Gwendolen is perfectly disgraceful. It is almost as bad as the way Gwendolen flirts with you.

Jack I am in love with Gwendolen. I have come up to town expressly to propose to her.

Algernon I thought you had come up for pleasure. I call that business.

Jack (*crossing to the mirror to adjust his jacket*) How utterly unromantic you are.

Algernon (*following him*) It's very romantic to be in love but I don't see anything romantic about a definite proposal. (*He breaks away to* C) But if you are absolutely determined to propose then you had better come to my flat this afternoon. Aunt Augusta and Gwendolen are coming to tea.

Jack I can't propose with Lady Bracknell present.

Algernon My dear fellow, you can rely on me to arrange it so that you and Gwendolen will be alone together. (*Taking a stick from the stand*) Though I doubt if you will ever marry her.

Jack (*swinging round to face Algernon*) Why on earth do you say that?

Algernon Because Gwendolen is my first cousin and before I allow you to marry her you will have to clear up the whole question of Cecily. (*He pushes the stick firmly into the stand*)

Jack (*turning away from Algernon*) Cecily? I don't know anyone by the name of Cecily.

Algernon (*taking a cigarette case out of his pocket and opening it*) The last time you dined with me you left a cigarette case in the smoking-room.

Jack (*turning to face Algernon*) Do you mean to say you have had my cigarette case all this time?

Algernon (*opening the case and examining the inside*) Ah! Now I look at the inscription inside I see it's not yours after all.

Jack Of course it's mine!

Jack reaches for the cigarette case which Algernon holds out of his reach

You've seen me with it a hundred times.

Algernon (*turning to Jack*) But this isn't your cigarette case. This case is a present from someone called Cecily and you just said you don't know anyone of that name.

Jack Well if you must know, Cecily happens to be my aunt.

Algernon Your aunt!

Jack Yes, and a charming old lady she is too. Lives in Tunbridge Wells. Just give it back to me, Algy.

He moves over and tries to get the case out of Algernon's hand. As Jack advances Algernon dodges behind him to his R

Algernon But why does she call herself "little Cecily" if she's your aunt and lives in Tunbridge Wells? (*He reads the inscription in the case*) "From little Cecily with her fondest love"!

Jack Some aunts are tall, some aunts are not tall. Surely that is something an aunt can decide for herself. For heaven's sake give me back my cigarette case.

He makes a sudden grab but Algernon again dodges behind him to his L *below the table* LC

Algernon But why does your aunt call you her uncle? "From little Cecily with her fondest love to her dear Uncle Jack." Besides, your name isn't Jack at all, it's Ernest.

Jack It is not Ernest, it is Jack.

Algernon (*crossing to face him*) But you have always told me that it was Ernest. I have introduced you to everyone as Ernest. You answer to the name of Ernest. In fact you are the most earnest-looking person I have ever seen in my life.

Jack Well, my name is Ernest in town and Jack in the country and the cigarette case was given to me in the country.

Algernon But that still doesn't account for the fact that your little aunt Cecily who lives in Tunbridge Wells calls you her Uncle Jack. Why don't you just tell me the truth? (*He pauses*) I have always suspected you of being a confirmed and secret Bunburyist and now I am quite sure of it.

Jack Bunburyist? What do you mean by Bunburyist?

Algernon I will reveal the meaning of that expression as soon as you are kind enough to inform me why you are Ernest in town and Jack in the country.

Jack Well give me my cigarette case first.

Algernon Here. (*He hands him the cigarette case then crosses to* LC *to sit in the chair* L *of the table*) Now produce your explanation; and do make it improbable.

Jack crosses to R *of the table, then moves downstage to* C

Jack There is nothing improbable about my explanation at all. In fact it's very ordinary. Old Mr Thomas Cardew, who adopted me when I was a little boy, made me guardian to his granddaughter, Miss Cecily Cardew, in his will. Cecily lives at my place in the country under the charge of her admirable governess Miss Prism.

Algernon But why are you Ernest in town and Jack in the country?

Jack (*moving upstage towards the chair* R *of the table*) As Cecily's guardian I have to adopt a very high moral tone on all subjects. And as a high moral tone can hardly be said to be very conducive to either one's health or happiness, in order to get up to town I have always pretended to have a younger brother by the name of Ernest who lives in the Albany, and gets into the most dreadful scrapes. That, my dear Algy, is the whole truth pure and simple.

Algernon (*moving* L *then turning to face Jack*) I was quite right in saying you were a Bunburyist. In fact you are one of the most advanced Bunburyists I know.

Jack What on earth is a Bunburyist?

Algernon Anyone who uses Mr Bunbury.

Jack And who is Mr Bunbury?

Algernon (*pushing Jack into the chair* L *of the table*) Bunbury is the perfect excuse. (*He puts one leg on the chair* R *of the table*)

Music No. 3: Bunburying

(*Singing*)   I have invented a sick old friend
Who's forever and eternally ill
So whenever I want to leave some place
Poor Bunbury catches a chill.
You have invented a brother
So you can come up to town when you choose
And it didn't take you long to discover
It's a marvellous deception to use.

He approaches the dummy LC *and treats it as Aunt Augusta*

If you've got an Aunt Augusta
Who insists the family muster
For the same old boring dinner every week
You've got to find a reason
Some kind of social treason
To escape from all that table hide and seek.

But what can a person say
That will avoid a confrontation
And let him get away
A martyr to obligation.

Jack (*speaking*) What?
Algernon   He goes Bunburying, Bunburying

As he sings the words "Bunburying Bunburying" a Mother and Daughter enter L *and pass behind the shop window. The Daughter stops to look in through the glass partition of the door. Algernon crosses up to the girl as the Mother returns to retrieve her Daughter and lead her off. Algernon blows a kiss as she departs, revealing that Bunburying has everything to do with pursuing the fair sex*

It's the only way I know that a gentleman can find
To do the better things on his gentle-manly-mind
His gentle-manly-mind.

As the girl exits R, *Algernon moves to the other dummy* R *with the Norfolk jacket and treats it as his Uncle George*

If your presence is requested
By old George who has invested

He puts his hand around the dummy's shoulder

A million something pounds on Highgate Hill
These cranky old recluses
Must have the right excuses

He picks up a large hat

Or you'll never get a penny in their will.

He rams the hat down on the dummy's head

               But what does a fellow do
               In that kind of situation
               And still get left some money
               In kind remuneration
               He goes

Jack   Bunburying. (*Rising and crossing to* LC)
Algernon   Yes Bunburying.
               It's the only way I know that a gentleman can find
               To do the better things on his gentle-manly-mind
               His gentle-manly-mind.

Algernon picks up his stick then turns to face Jack

               But if I got an invitation
               To visit that young relation

He points his stick into the distance

               Who lives in Shropshire at your country place
               If Cecily is pretty

When he hears the name Cecily, Jack crosses behind Algernon towards the R
alcove, summoning two Assistants

  They enter with his hat and cane. The Assistants hand them to Jack and one
  moves to open the C *door for him while Mr Lake enters from the alcove to*
  see Jack off

               I'll leave this crowded city
               To seek a little natural style and grace
               I just need her home address
               And her uncle's approbation

He appeals to Jack

Jack (*speaking*) Never.

  He exits through the C *door*

Algernon   And I'll take the next express
               To her nearest country station

A Shop Assistant enters R *carrying a pile of shirts and crosses* L

               I'll go Bunburying, Bunburying

As the Assistant passes him Algernon sends the pile of shirts flying as he sings
the first "Bunburying". The other two Assistants rush to pick them up

               It's the only way I know that a gentleman can find
               To do the better things on his gentle-manly-mind
               His gentle-manly-mind.

One Assistant takes the shirts off while Mr Lake makes a sign to the other two
Assistants to hand Algernon his hat, gloves and cane

Music No. 3A: Scene change

Algernon moves downstage as the Lights fade upstage. The Shop Assistants change the furniture from the tailor's shop to Algy's flat. Downstage Lane and a Servant help Algernon out of his day coat into his smoking jacket and take his hat, gloves and cane off

SCENE 3

The morning room in Algernon's flat in Half Moon Street

The furnishings are not luxurious and give an indication of Algernon's financial situation. There are doors up R and L. UC is a large picture window with a magnificent view of Central London in 1895. A table C is laid for tea, there is a high-backed settee L of the table. Another table stands R with cigarettes etc.

When the Lights come up, Lane is discovered behind the settee adjusting cushions and Algernon behind the round table RC with a plate with one cucumber sandwich on it in one hand and a half-eaten sandwich in the other

Algernon Lane, have you got any more cucumber sandwiches for Lady Bracknell?

Lane (*moving to* L *of the table*) No sir, I had to go down to the market twice before anyone would give me credit for half a cucumber—(*he pauses*)—there being no ready money available this morning, sir.

Algernon returns the plate to the table, where the tray stands, all laid with tea things for four and plates of bread and butter

Algernon She seldom takes more than two anyway.

Lane But there is only one sandwich left, sir.

Algernon (*firmly*) That will be all, Lane.

Lane Very good, sir.

Lane exits R

Algernon gets up and walks around the table inspecting the last cucumber sandwich

Lane enters

Lane Mr Ernest Worthing.

Jack enters

Lane exits R taking Jack's hat and gloves

Algernon Come in, Ernest, or should I call you Jack. Whoever you are please don't touch the cucumber sandwiches, they've been made especially for Aunt Augusta. (*He picks up the last cucumber sandwich and eats it*)

Jack But you are eating the last sandwich yourself.

Algernon That is quite a different matter. She is my aunt.

He picks up the plate of bread and butter from the table and offers it to Jack who moves to the settee

Have some bread and butter. Gwendolen is absolutely devoted to bread and butter.

Jack takes a slice of bread and butter and starts eating

Jack And very good bread and butter it is too.

Jack sits on the settee, but at the sound of the bell he rises again

Algernon Ah, that must be Aunt Augusta.

Jack crosses with his plate to the tea table

Now if I get her out of the way for ten minutes so that you can propose to Gwendolen, may I dine with you tonight at Willis's?

Jack I suppose so.

He puts the plate on the table and stands by the chair, while Algernon moves to the DS end of the settee

Lane enters C

Lane (*announcing*) Lady Bracknell and Miss Fairfax.

Algernon moves forward to greet them.

Lady Bracknell and Gwendolen enter C

Lane exits

Algernon approaches Lady Bracknell to kiss her hand

Lady Bracknell (*moving* C) Good-afternoon, Algernon. I hope you are behaving well. (*She takes Algernon's hand and moves* LC)

Algernon I am feeling very well thank you, Aunt Augusta.

Lady Bracknell That is not quite the same thing. In fact the two rarely go together.

Lady Bracknell hands her parasol to Algernon who places it at the head of the settee. She crosses to below the settee, as Gwendolen descends the stairs into the room to C. Lady Bracknell bows to Jack with icy coldness

Good-afternoon, Mr Worthing.

Jack Good-afternoon, Lady Bracknell. I trust you are well.

Algernon Dear me, you are smart. (*He kisses Gwendolen on the cheek*)

Lady Bracknell sits on the settee

Gwendolen I am always smart. (*She turns towards Jack*) Am I not, Mr Worthing?

Jack You are quite perfect, Miss Fairfax.

Gwendolen Oh, I hope that I am not that. It would leave no room for development.

Gwendolen moves to the chair R *of the table and sits. Algernon moves to sit beside Lady Bracknell on the settee*

Lady Bracknell I'm sorry if we are a little late, Algernon, but we were obliged to call on dear Lady Harbury.

Lane enters R, *carrying a teapot, which he puts on the table*

I hadn't been there since her poor husband's death. I never saw a woman so altered; she looks quite twenty years younger. And now I'll have a cup of tea and one of those nice cucumber sandwiches you promised me.

Lane fingers a cup or two, then moves back to the door

Algernon Certainly, Aunt Augusta. (*He moves to the tea table and picks up the empty plate in horror*) Good heavens! Lane! Why are there no cucumber sandwiches? I ordered them specially.
Lane (*moving to him; gravely*) There were no cucumbers in the market this morning, sir, even though I went down twice.
Algernon No cucumbers!
Lane No, sir. Not even for ready money, sir.
Algernon That will do, Lane.
Lane Very good, sir.

Lane takes the plate from Algernon and exits R

Algernon (*pouring out tea*) I am greatly distressed, Aunt Augusta, about there being no cucumbers—not even for ready money.
Lady Bracknell It really doesn't matter, Algernon. I had some crumpets with Lady Harbury, who seems to me to be living entirely for pleasure these days.

Algernon returns to the settee with two cups of tea. He hands Lady Bracknell a cup then sits R *of her. Jack picks up two cups of tea and takes one to Gwendolen*

Algernon I am afraid, Aunt Augusta, I shall have to give up the pleasure of dining with you tonight after all.
Lady Bracknell (*frowning*) I hope not, Algernon. It would put my table completely out. Your uncle would have to dine upstairs.
Algernon I need hardly say it's a terrible disappointment to me, but the fact is, I have just had a telegram to say that my poor friend Bunbury is very ill again.

Algernon exchanges glances with Jack behind Lady Bracknell

They seem to think I should be with him.
Lady Bracknell This Mr Bunbury seems to suffer from curiously bad health.
Algernon Yes, poor Bunbury is a dreadful invalid.
Lady Bracknell I consider it high time that Mr Bunbury made up his mind whether he is going to live or die. This shilly-shallying with the question is absurd. I would be obliged if you would ask him not to have a relapse on

Saturday. It is my last reception and I am relying on you to arrange my music for me.

Algernon takes Lady Bracknell's tea-cup, rises and puts her cup and his own on the table behind the settee

Algernon I'll speak to Bunbury, Aunt Augusta, if he is still conscious. But I think I can promise you that he'll be all right on Saturday. Selecting the music for your reception has presented particular problems, but I will run over the programme that I have drawn out if you will kindly come into the next room for a moment.

Lady Bracknell Thank you, Algernon. It is very thoughtful of you.

Lady Bracknell rises and Algernon hands her her parasol

I'm sure the programme will be delightful after a few expurgations. Gwendolen, you will accompany me.

Gwendolen Certainly, Mamma. (*She remains seated*)

Lady Bracknell and Algernon exit into the library R

Music No. 4: The Importance of Being Ernest/One Love

Jack, with his cup, follows Algernon towards the exit, then puts his cup on the table behind the settee and moves round to the front of the settee. Gwendolen rises and puts her cup on the tea table

Jack	A charming day it's been Miss Fairfax
	Quite warm for the time of year.
Gwendolen	Pray don't remind me
	The sun is behind me
	It just makes me nervous to hear.
	I thought you had something
	Important to tell me.
Jack	I do have something to say.

Jack and Gwendolen meet C

	I've admired you since I met you
	I hope I'm not being too bold.

He retreats a step

Gwendolen	No please do proceed
	Say whatever you need
	The truth has to be told
Jack	I must say it now.

He moves closer

Gwendolen	I do hope you will
	For Mamma may return quite soon.

As Jack crosses UC *to look off, Gwendolen moves* LC. *Jack then comes down on her* R

(*Speaking*) She has a way of coming back suddenly into a room that I have often had to speak to her about.

Jack (*singing*) One love here in my heart
One dream when we're apart.
Oh I need you, adore you, I love you.
Darling, please say you'll be mine
Darling, please tell me you're mine.

Jack moves behind Gwendolen to her left

One love tender and true
One dream only of you
Oh I need you, adore you, I love you.
Darling, please say you'll be mine.
Darling, please tell me you're mine.

Jack takes her hand

Give me your hand, sweet valentine
Give me your lips red as the wine
Say that you love me set my heart free
Tell me you'll share your whole life with me.

Gwendolen (*speaking*) The moment Algernon first mentioned to me that he had a friend called Ernest, I knew I was destined to love you.

Jack You really love me, Gwendolen?

Gwendolen Passionately!

Jack You don't know how happy you've made me.

Gwendolen (*about to kiss Jack*) My own Ernest!

Jack (*breaking off the kiss*) But you don't really mean to say that you couldn't love me if my name wasn't Ernest?

Gwendolen But your name is Ernest. (*She releases him*)

Jack (*breaking away to* L *of the settee*) Yes, I know it is, but personally, darling, I don't care for the name of Ernest ... I don't think the name suits me at all.

Gwendolen (*sitting at the* R *end of the settee*) It suits you perfectly. It produces vibrations.

Jack (*sitting at the* L *end of the settee beside her*) But there are lots of other much nicer names. I think, er, Jack, for example, is a really charming name.

Gwendolen (*speaking*) Jack, Jack, it sounds like the quack
Of a duck in a pond at the zoo.
(*Singing*) No I assure you, my darling,
That's one name that will never ever do.

Gwendolen rises and moves away to C

The importance of being Ernest
Is something I'm certain about.

Jack   The Charles'?
Gwendolen   Leave me cold.

Jack	And the Harrys?
Gwendolen	Too old.
Jack	The Percys?
Gwendolen	And I don't agree
	I knew my intention
	The moment they mentioned
	The name of Ernest to me

Gwendolen circles behind the tea table and comes DR *of it*

	The importance of being Ernest
	Is something I'll never forget.
Jack	My name
Gwendolen	Is divine
	And it goes well with mine
Jack	It sounds
Gwendolen	So honest and free (*She moves* C)
	I'll never discover
	True love with another
	I've made up my mind you see.

Gwendolen sits beside Jack who rises and moves C

Jack (*speaking*) Gwendolen, I must get christened at once. (*He hastily corrects himself*) I mean we must get married at once. There is no time to be lost. (*He moves* UC *towards the exit*)

Gwendolen (*rising*) Married, Mr Worthing?

Jack (*moving to face Gwendolen*) Well . . . surely. You know that I love you, and you led me to believe, Miss Fairfax, that you were not absolutely indifferent to me.

Gwendolen I adore you. But you haven't proposed to me yet. Nothing at all has been said about marriage. The subject has not even been touched on.

Jack (*moving towards Gwendolen*) Well . . . may I propose to you now?

Gwendolen I think this is an admirable opportunity. And to spare you any possible disappointment, Mr Worthing, it's only fair to tell you quite frankly beforehand that I am fully determined to accept you. (*She sits on the settee*)

Jack Gwendolen!

Gwendolen (*as though she hardly knows him*) Yes, Mr Worthing, what have you got to say to me?

Jack You know what I have got to say to you.

Gwendolen (*very reasonably*) Yes, but you don't say it.

Jack Gwendolen.

Gwendolen Yes Mr Worthing?

Jack (*singing*) One love here in my heart
    One dream when we're apart
    Oh I need you, adore you, I love you.

Jack kneels at her feet

    Darling, will you marry me

Darling, please do marry me.

Gwendolen (*speaking*) Of course I will, Ernest. (*She puts her arms around his neck*)

Jack My dearest Gwendolen.

Jack } Give me your hand, sweet valentine.
Gwendolen / Give me your lips red as the wine.
Say that you love me—set my heart free
Tell me you'll share your whole life with me.

Gwendolen One love tender and true
One dream only of you
Jack Oh I need you, adore you, I love you
Gwendolen Darling at last you are mine.

Jack and Gwendolen kiss

(*Speaking*) What wonderfully blue eyes you have, Ernest! They are quite, quite blue. I hope you will always look at me just like that, especially when there are other people present.

Lady Bracknell enters

Lady Bracknell Mr Worthing!

Jack tries to get up. Gwendolen restrains him. Lady Bracknell comes DC

Rise, sir, from this semi-recumbent posture, it is most indecorous.

Gwendolen Mamma! I must beg you to retire. This is no place for you. Besides, Mr Worthing has not quite finished yet.

Lady Bracknell Finished what, may I ask?

Gwendolen and Jack rise together

Gwendolen I am engaged to Mr Worthing, Mamma.

Lady Bracknell Pardon me, you are not engaged to anyone. When you do become engaged to someone, I, or your father, should his health permit him, will inform you of the fact. An engagement should come on a young girl as a surprise, pleasant or unpleasant, as the case may be. It is hardly a matter that she could be allowed to arrange for herself. Pray leave us, Mr Worthing. I wish to speak to my daughter alone. (*She follows Jack with a stern look until he has left the room*)

Jack exits

Lady Bracknell turns to Gwendolen who moves downstage

Music No. 5: Your Engagement

(*Singing*) Parents have to be so careful, my dear,
When it comes to choosing a man.
Just like everything else in this world
One must have an organized plan.

Lady Bracknell walks Gwendolen across the stage by degrees to RC

The age is important and the style of his clothes
No mother would allow any clash of those.
But income is always at the top of my list
How much how safe and does it really exist.

I'd leave education absolutely to chance.
You teach them too much and, well, just look at France.
They'd never have suffered from republican rule
If they'd had cold showers and cricket at school.

Lady Bracknell crosses to the L side of Gwendolen

My child, your engagement will be
Arranged by me very carefully.
My child, nothing can proceed
Until your father and I have agreed.

Lady Bracknell moves away below settee L

He should be related to a title or two
As long as there's nothing suspiciously new.
A duke or a marquis with a nice stately hall,
Though royalty of course would be best of all.

Gwendolen moves to Lady Bracknell

My child, your engagement will be
Arranged by me very carefully.
My child, nothing can proceed
Until your father and I have agreed.

His house here in London will become your address
The meaning of that, child, I hardly need stress.
Just think of the problem if you found yourself tied
To one on the right street but on the wrong side

Lady Bracknell crosses to C

My child, your engagement will be
Arranged by me very carefully.
My child, nothing can proceed
Until your father and I have agreed.

(*Speaking*) And now I have a few questions to put to Mr Worthing. (*She walks across and rings the bell then moves to below the table* RC) While I am making these enquiries, you, Gwendolen, will wait in the carriage.
Gwendolen But Mamma——

Lane enters

Lady Bracknell Tell Mr Worthing I wish to see him.
Lane Yes, my lady.

Lane exits

Lady Bracknell Gwendolen, the carriage!

Jack enters

He blows a tender kiss to Gwendolen behind Lady Bracknell's back as she walks to the door. Lady Bracknell turns round just as Gwendolen is returning the blown kiss

Gwendolen, the carriage!

Gwendolen Yes, Mamma.

Gwendolen exits

Lady Bracknell (*crossing to the settee and sitting*) You can take a seat, Mr Worthing. (*She looks in her handbag for a notebook and pencil*)

Jack (*moving downstage to below the chair L of the table*) Thank you, Lady Bracknell, I prefer standing.

Lady Bracknell (*pencil and notebook in hand*) I feel bound to tell you that you are not down on my list of eligible young men. However, I am quite ready to enter your name, should your answers be what a really affectionate mother requires. How old are you?

Jack Twenty-nine.

Lady Bracknell A very good age to be married. I have always been of the opinion that a man who desires to get married should know either everything or nothing. Which do you know?

Jack (*after some hesitation*) I know nothing, Lady Bracknell.

Lady Bracknell I am pleased to hear it. I do not approve of anything that tampers with natural ignorance. The whole theory of modern education is radically unsound. Fortunately, in England, education produces no effect whatsoever. What is your income?

Jack Between seven and eight thousand a year.

Lady Bracknell (*making a note in her book*) In land, or in investments?

Jack In investments, chiefly.

Lady Bracknell That is satisfactory.

Jack I have a country house with some land attached to it, about fifteen hundred acres; but I don't depend on it for my real income.

Lady Bracknell A country house! (*She makes a note*) You also have a town house, I hope? A girl with a simple, unspoiled nature, like Gwendolen, could hardly be expected to reside in the country.

Jack I own a house in Belgrave Square.

Lady Bracknell What number in Belgrave Square?

Jack One hundred and forty-nine.

Lady Bracknell (*shaking her head*) The unfashionable side. I knew there was something. (*She makes a note, closes her book and puts it away*) Now to minor matters. Are your parents living?

Jack I have lost both my parents.

Lady Bracknell To lose one parent, Mr Worthing, may be regarded as a misfortune; to lose both looks like carelessness. Who was your father? He was evidently a man of some wealth. Was he born in what the Radical papers call the purple of commerce, or did he rise from the ranks of the aristocracy?

Jack I am afraid I really don't know. The fact is Lady Bracknell, I said I
had lost my parents. It would be nearer the truth to say that my parents
seem to have lost me . . . I don't actually know who I am by birth . . . well,
I was found.

Lady Bracknell Found!

Jack The late Thomas Cardew, a very charitable old gentleman, found me
and gave me the name of Worthing because he happened to have a first-
class ticket for Worthing in his pocket at the time.

Lady Bracknell Where did the charitable gentleman who had a first-class
ticket for this seaside resort find you?

Jack (*gravely*) In a handbag.

Lady Bracknell A handbag?

Jack (*very seriously*) Yes, Lady Bracknell. I was in a handbag—a somewhat
large, black leather handbag, with handles to it.

Lady Bracknell In what locality did this Mr Thomas Cardew come across
this handbag?

Jack In the cloakroom at Victoria Station. It was given to him in mistake
for his own.

Lady Bracknell The cloakroom at Victoria Station?

Jack Yes. The Brighton line.

Lady Bracknell The line is immaterial. (*She rises*) Mr Worthing. I confess I
feel somewhat bewildered by what you have just told me. To be born, or
at any rate bred, in a handbag, whether it had handles or not, seems to me
to display a contempt for the ordinary decencies of family life that
reminds one of the worst excesses of the French Revolution. A cloakroom
at a railway station could hardly be regarded as an assured basis for a
recognized position in good society.

Jack Lady Bracknell, may I ask you then, what would you advise me to do?

Lady Bracknell Advise you to do, Mr Worthing?

Music No. 5A: Your Engagement (continuation)

(*Singing*)   I strongly advise you to acquire some relations
                 By scouring the cloakrooms of all the main stations.
                 In your case I'm certain that a parent or two
                 Is not just belated it's long overdue.

She crosses back to LC

                 You cannot imagine that Lord Bracknell and I
                 Would dream of permitting such a dubious tie.
                 No gel in our family who's been brought up with care
                 Would marry a parcel no matter how rare.

She advances on Jack

                 Mr Worthing, this engagement can't be.
                 Lord Bracknell and I could never agree.
                 Which leaves just one thing to say
                 And that, Mr Worthing, is simply good-day.

She moves to the settee to collect her parasol

> Good-day.

She moves upstage to C *exit then turns when she reaches the door and delivers her final word*

> Good-day.

Lady Bracknell exits

Algernon enters from the library singing "Here Comes The Bride"

Jack sits at the L *end of the settee and Algernon comes to* US *end of the settee*

Jack For goodness sake stop singing that ghastly tune.

Algernon (*stopping singing*) Didn't it go off all right, old boy? You don't mean to say Gwendolen refused you?

Jack Oh Gwendolen is right as a trivet. As far as she is concerned, we are engaged. But her mother is a perfect Gorgon.

Algernon (*moving to the settee and perching at the* R *end*) By the way, did you tell Gwendolen the truth about being Ernest in town and Jack in the country?

Jack Certainly not.

Algernon But what about your brother? What about the profligate Ernest?

Jack Oh, before the end of the week I shall have got rid of him. I'll say he died in Paris of apoplexy. Lots of people die of apoplexy, quite suddenly, don't they?

Algernon (*rising and moving down to* C) Yes, but it's hereditary, my dear fellow. It's the sort of thing that runs in families. You had better say it was a severe chill.

Jack Very well then. My poor brother Ernest will be carried off suddenly, in Paris, by a severe chill. That gets rid of him.

Algernon (*moving to the settee and sitting at the* R *end beside Jack*) But I thought you said Miss Cardew was a little bit too interested in your poor brother Ernest? Won't she feel his loss a good deal?

Jack Oh that's all right. Cecily is not a silly romantic girl, she's got a capital appetite, goes for long walks and pays no attention at all to her lessons.

Algernon I still want to meet Cecily.

Jack I will take very good care you never do. She is excessively pretty, and only just eighteen.

Algernon Have you told Gwendolen that you have an excessively pretty ward who is just eighteen?

Jack Cecily and Gwendolen are certain to be extremely great friends. I'll bet you anything you like that half an hour after they've met they will be calling each other sister.

Algernon (*rising*) Women only do that when they have called each other a lot of other things first. (*He moves to the table to eat more bread and butter*) Now, my dear boy, if we want to get a good table at Willis's we really must go and dress. I'm hungry.

Gwendolen enters

She moves to Algernon as Jack rises

Gwendolen!

Gwendolen turns Algernon round

Gwendolen Algy, kindly turn your back. I have something very particular to say to Mr Worthing.

Gwendolen moves across to face Jack

Music No. 5B: One Love (underscore)

Jack My own darling!

Gwendolen Ernest, we may never be married. From the expression on Mamma's face I fear we never shall. But although she may prevent us from becoming man and wife, nothing that she can possibly do can alter my devotion to you.

Jack (*moving to her left and taking her hands in his*) My dearest Gwendolen!

Gwendolen The story of your romantic origin as related to me by Mamma has stirred the deeper fibres of my nature. Your Christian name has an irresistible fascination. (*She lets go of Jack's hands to take out a notebook and pencil*) Your town address at the Albany I have. What is your address in the country?

Jack The Manor House, Woolton, Hertfordshire.

Algernon, who has been listening carefully, smiles to himself and writes the address in his notebook, then rings for Lane by pressing the bell US *and comes down to the table to finish his tea*

Gwendolen There is a good postal service I suppose? It may be necessary to do something desperate. I will communicate with you daily.

Jack My own one!

Jack and Gwendolen kiss

Gwendolen Algy, you may turn round now.

Algernon Thanks, I've turned round already.

Jack You will let me see you to your carriage, my own darling?

Gwendolen Certainly.

Jack and Gwendolen exit upstage

Lane enters

Lane Yes, sir.

Algernon (*putting down his teacup*) Where is the *Railway Guide*, Lane?

Lane Here, sir.

Lane takes the book from the shelf and hands it to Algernon

Algernon (*moving downstage, turning the pages*) Let me see. Warminster, Wolverham, Wolverhampton, Woolton, Hertfordshire, ten thirty-five, twelve forty-two, and four-fifty. Tomorrow, Lane, I'm going Bunburying. (*He hands the "Railway Guide" back to Lane*)

Lane (*replacing the Guide in the bookshelf and returning to Algernon*) Yes sir.
Algernon I shall probably not be back till Monday. Put out my dress
clothes, my smoking jacket, and all the usual Bunbury suits and hats and
things. You see, Lane . . .
Lane Yes, sir.

Music No. 6: Bunburying (reprise)

Two Maids enter with Algernon's day jacket, hat, gloves and cane

*Lane assists Algernon out of his smoking jacket and into his day jacket and
hands him his gloves and cane*

One Maid takes the smoking jacket from Lane and both Maids exit

Algernon   I can't get an invitation
                    To visit that young relation
                    Who likes long walks and shares my appetite.
Lane (*speaking*) I'm sorry to hear it, sir.
Algernon   But now I know she's pretty
                    I'll leave this crowded city
                    To save poor Bunbury from his dreadful plight.
Lane (*speaking*) Of course sir.
Algernon   I've got her home address,
                    The perfect destination,
                    So I'll take the next express
                    To her nearest country station.
                    I'm going Bunburying, Bunburying.
                    It's the only way I know a gentleman can find

*As the Lights fade upstage, Servants enter to remove morning room
furniture and bring on garden furniture for the next scene*

                    To do the better things on his gentle-manly-mind
                    And Cecily is on my mind.

Algernon exits

Music 6A: Scene change

SCENE 4

In the grounds of the Manor House, Woolton

*It is July and the leaves on the trees and shrubs are looking very green in the
sunlight. A garden table, covered with books, is set under a large tree L. There
is a hammock chair, and a little below this is a wicker table with more books. A
garden bench is downstage R. The whole appearance of the garden conveys the
impression of a hot summer afternoon*

*As the CURTAIN rises, Miss Prism is discovered seated at the table. Cecily is
directing the Servants as they rehearse a tableau for the local garden fête.
They are partly dressed as heroic figures of the British Empire—Queen*

*Victoria, Britannia, Nelson, Florence Nightingale, John Bull and Disraeli.
Cecily is standing* DRC *of the group of Servants who are carrying all their
props: telescope, lantern, scroll, orb, trident etc.*

Cecily Do stand up straight, Mabel, I'm sure Florence Nightingale never
slouched. A bit more authority, Henry, Disraeli was our Prime Minister.

Miss Prism Cecily, you must end your rehearsal, it is time to resume your
lessons.

Cecily But the costumes only arrived this morning, Miss Prism, and it is
vital that we rehearse our tableau for the fête on Saturday.

Miss Prism, who has been opening the school books on the table LC *crosses to
Cecily*

Miss Prism The glories of the British Empire will have to wait until this
afternoon, Cecily. We must commence your German lesson. (*She crosses
back to the table and sits in the* UL *chair*)

Cecily But I don't like German. I know perfectly well I look quite plain
after every German lesson.

Miss Prism You know how anxious your guardian is that you should
improve yourself in every way.

Cecily moves to the table L *and turns upstage to address the Servants and
members of her Empire League*

Cecily Very well. The full dress rehearsal will take place this afternoon at
three o'clock when everyone must wear their full costumes. That will be
all for now.

Servants Yes, miss.

The Servants go off

Cecily (*crossing* R) Dear Uncle Jack is so very serious! Sometimes he is so
serious that I think he cannot be well.

Miss Prism rises, crosses to Cecily to lead her back and seat her R *of the table,
sitting herself in the* US *chair*

Miss Prism Cecily! I am surprised at you. Mr Worthing has many troubles
in his life. Idle merriment and triviality would be out of place in his
conversation. You must remember his constant anxiety about that
unfortunate young man, his brother.

Cecily I have made numerous observations about his brother in my diary.
(*She picks up her diary*)

Miss Prism I don't believe you should mention him at all. According to
your guardian he is irretrievably weak and vacillating.

Cecily Perhaps that is why I find I have to write about him at least twice
every day.

Miss Prism I advise you to ignore him in future. Diaries are not necessary,
Cecily. Memory is the diary that we should all carry about with us.

Cecily Yes, but it usually chronicles the things that could never have happened. I believe that memory is responsible for nearly all the three-volume novels that our local bookshop sends us. (*She puts the diary down on the table*)

Miss Prism Do not speak slightingly of the three-volume novel, Cecily. I wrote one myself in earlier days.

Cecily (*rising to join Miss Prism above the table*) Did you really, Miss Prism? How wonderfully clever you are! And was your novel ever published?

Miss Prism (*very sadly*) Alas! No. The manuscript was unfortunately abandoned! I use the word in the sense of lost or mislaid.

Cecily re-seats herself in the chair R of the table

But my work as an author has nothing whatsoever to do with your lessons.

Cecily starts to write in her diary

Cecily, do put away that diary. It is completely unnecessary for a girl to keep a diary.

Cecily On the contrary, Miss Prism. I need a diary to write down all the wonderful secrets of my life as they occur. If I didn't put them down immediately I should probably forget all about them.

Music No. 7: I Must Write That Down Before I Forget

Cecily rises and moves round the table to show her diary to Miss Prism

(*Singing*)   I start at the very top
                With the day and the date, full stop.
                Leaving the whole of the page
                Like a small empty stage
                For the day's events to be played on.

Cecily waltzes away to the garden bench R

Miss Prism (*speaking*) Cecily! We must proceed with your German lesson. (*Very firmly*) Open your grammar at page fifteen.

Cecily sits on the bench and sings

Cecily   I really don't want to learn horrid old German
                Just thinking about it can make me upset.

Miss Prism (*speaking*) We will repeat yesterday's exercise.

Cecily   It's slow and it's dull like a bad Sunday Sermon

She pauses as though she's just said something wonderful

                Oh I must write that down before I forget.

She starts writing in her diary

                I must write that down before I forget.

Cecily rises and moves C

> I'd much rather write about wonderful things
> Than solve the equations that you always set,
> Like the moment at daybreak when every bird sings.
> (*Pausing*) Oh I must write that down before I forget.
> I must write that down before I forget.

Cecily dances around with her diary as Miss Prism pursues her with the German book, leading her back to the table. They both sit

Miss Prism (*interrupting to bring some sanity into the discussion*)
> Learning is essential to fill up the mind
> To stop foolish chatter and things of that kind,
> And German has always been vital to know
> Without it, my child, where on earth could you go?

Cecily   I think about dear Uncle Jack every day
> And how that bad brother keeps making him fret
> I know I could change him if I—er—we had our way.

Cecily rises, snatches the diary from Miss Prism and goes to sit on the bench and write in her diary

> Oh I must write that down before I forget.
> I must write that down before I forget.

Miss Prism rises, crosses to behind the bench

Miss Prism   Young men are never that easy to change,
> I recall one I tried hard to arrange,
> But one day a good man will capture your heart

Miss Prism places the German book on top of the diary

> And that's when your German will set you apart
Cecily   I must leave some space for what still has to come
> For no-one can know what fate's caught in his net
> A prince might be passing and stop here in fun.

Cecily rises to C *with the diary, leaving Miss Prism at* DSR *of the bench*

> Oh I must write that down,
> I must write that down,
> I must write that down before I forget.

Cecily ends up seated in the chair R *of the table*

Dr Chasuble enters

Miss Prism (*moving to the front of the bench*) Dr Chasuble, this is indeed a pleasure.

Dr Chasuble And how are we this morning? Miss Prism, you are I trust, well?

Cecily (*rising to face Dr Chasuble*) Miss Prism has just been complaining of a slight headache. I think it would do her so much good to have a short stroll with you in the park, Dr Chasuble.

Miss Prism Cecily, I have not mentioned anything about a headache.

Cecily (*crossing Dr Chasuble to join Miss Prism*) No, dear Miss Prism, I know that, but I felt instinctively that you had a headache. Indeed I was thinking about that, and not about my German lesson, when the rector came in.

Dr Chasuble (*taking a pace or two towards them*) That is strange. Were I fortunate enough to be Miss Prism's pupil, I would hang upon her lips. I speak metaphorically. My metaphor was drawn from the bees. Ahem! Mr Worthing, I suppose, has not returned from town yet?

Miss Prism We do not expect him till Monday afternoon.

Dr Chasuble Ah yes, he usually likes to spend his Sunday in London. He is not one of those whose sole aim is enjoyment, as, by all accounts, that unfortunate young man his brother seems to be. But I must not disturb Egeria and her pupil any longer. (*He turns to depart*)

Miss Prism Egeria? My name is Laetitia, Doctor.

Dr Chasuble (*bowing and raising his hat*) A classical allusion merely, drawn from the pagan authors. I shall see you both no doubt at Evensong?

Miss Prism (*crossing to Dr Chasuble*) I think, dear Doctor, I will have a stroll with you. I find I have a headache after all, and a walk might do me good.

Dr Chasuble With pleasure, Miss Prism, with pleasure. We might go as far as the school and back.

Miss Prism That would be delightful.

Miss Prism collects a parasol from the table L, *as Cecily sits at the table*

Cecily, you will read your Political Economy in my absence. The chapter on the Fall of the Rupee you may omit. It is somewhat too sensational for your young mind. Even these metallic problems have their melodramatic side.

Miss Prism exits with Dr Chasuble

Cecily rises to watch them go off, then returns to the chair above the table

Cecily (*picking up each book in turn and throwing it back on the table*) Horrid Political Economy! Horrid Geography! Horrid, horrid German!

Merriman enters carrying a card on a salver

Merriman A Mr Ernest Worthing has just driven over from the station. He has brought his luggage with him.

Cecily (*reading*) "Mr Ernest Worthing, B-four, The Albany, W." Uncle Jack's brother! Did you tell him my guardian was in town?

Merriman Yes, miss. He seemed very disappointed. I mentioned that you and Miss Prism were in the garden. He said he was anxious to speak to you privately for a moment.

Cecily Ask Mr Ernest Worthing to come here. I suppose you had better talk to the housekeeper about a room for him.

Merriman Yes, miss.

Merriman exits

Cecily I have never met any really wicked person before. I feel rather frightened. I am so afraid he will look just like everyone else.

Algernon enters, looking very debonair

He does!

Algernon (*raising his hat*) You must be my little cousin Cecily. (*He puts his hat on the table*)

Cecily (*rising to meet him* C) You are under some strange misapprehension. I am not little. In fact, I believe I am more than usually tall for my age.

Algernon is rather taken aback

But I am your cousin, Cecily. You, I see from your card, are Uncle Jack's brother, my cousin Ernest, my wicked cousin Ernest.

Algernon Oh! I am not really wicked at all, Cousin Cecily.

Cecily If you are not, then you have certainly been deceiving us all in a very inexcusable manner. I hope you have not been leading a double life, pretending to be wicked and being really good all the time. That would be hypocrisy.

Algernon (*looking at her in amazement*) Well, I, er, I have been rather reckless.

Cecily (*sitting in the chair above the table*) I am glad to hear it.

Algernon In fact, now you mention the subject, I have been very bad in my own small way.

Cecily I don't think you should be so proud of that, though I am sure it must have been very pleasant.

Algernon (*sitting in the chair* R *of the table*) It is much pleasanter being here with you.

Cecily I don't understand why you are here at all. Uncle Jack won't be back till Monday afternoon.

Algernon That is a great disappointment. I am obliged to return by the first train on Monday morning.

Cecily I think you had better wait till Uncle Jack arrives. He wants to speak to you about your emigrating.

Algernon (*startled*) My what?

Cecily Your emigrating. He has gone up to buy your outfit.

Algernon I certainly wouldn't let Jack buy my outfit. He has no taste in neckties at all.

Cecily I don't think you will require neckties. Uncle Jack is sending you to Australia.

Algernon Australia! (*He rises*) I'd sooner die.

Cecily That is one of the choices he is offering you. He said at dinner on Wednesday night that you would have to choose between this world, the next world and Australia.

Algernon (*moving to* C) This world is quite good enough for me, Cousin Cecily.

Cecily Yes, but are you good enough for it?

Music No. 8: I Need Someone to Rescue Me

Algernon (*speaking*) I'm afraid I'm not.

(*Singing*)   I'm just a bad and wicked man
Who's always refused to bend the knee
I've played too hard and paid the price
I need someone to rescue me.

(*Speaking*) Make me your mission, Cousin Cecily. (*He moves nearer to Cecily*)

Cecily I never undertake missions.

Algernon moves away from Cecily to try a different approach

Algernon (*singing*)   I'm just a ship without a sail
Lost and adrift on a stormy sea
No-one to guide me to my home
I need someone to rescue me.

(*Moving nearer to Cecily again; speaking*) Reform me, Cousin Cecily.

Cecily (*rising to cross Algernon and sit on the bench*) I'm afraid I have no time this afternoon.

Algernon (*singing*)   What will become of me today
If you refuse my plea? (*Turning to Cecily*)
What will become of me in time
If you won't rescue me?

Algernon tries yet another approach adopting an upright pose

Maybe I could reform myself
And start to live a better life
I'm sure I feel it working now.
(*Appealing to Cecily*)
Please do say that you agree.

(*Moving to the bench, speaking*) I do look a lot better, don't I?

Cecily I think you're looking a little worse.

Algernon That is because I'm hungry.

Cecily How thoughtless of me. I should have remembered that when one is going to lead an entirely new life one requires regular and wholesome meals. I will tell Merriman to prepare something for you immediately. (*She rises and moves upstage*)

Algernon Thank you. (*He moves to her*) Might I have a buttonhole first?

Cecily A carnation?

Algernon I'd sooner have a pink rose.

Cecily Why?

Algernon Because you are like a pink rose, Cousin Cecily.

Cecily (*moving away to behind the chair and facing away from him*) I don't think it can be right for you to talk to me like that. Miss Prism never says such things to me.

Algernon Then Miss Prism is a shortsighted old lady. (*He moves to her*)

(*Singing*)   It's hard to be a wicked man
Through fire and stormy sea.

Algernon turns her to face him

> All I need is one dear hand
> To save and comfort me.
>
> I need someone to help me change
> To break the spell and find the key
> An angel who will lead the way,
> I need you to rescue me.

(*Speaking*) You are the prettiest girl I've ever seen.

Algernon moves to kiss her but . . .

Merriman enters

Algernon moves away from Cecily to collect his hat and gloves

Cecily Merriman, show Mr Worthing to his room and ask Cook to prepare something for him urgently.

They turn to exit but Cecily pauses

I must collect my books.

Algernon gazes at her fondly for a moment then exits with Merriman into the house

Cecily takes C stage

Music No. 8A: I Must Write That Down

(*Singing*)   I wish Uncle Jack could have been here today
                     To see his poor brother show signs of regret.

Cecily gathers her books from the table then moves C

> I know I can change him if I have my way
> Oh I must write that down before I forget,
> I must write that down before I forget.

She exits running into the house

The Lights fade and the Servants enter to change the scene, moving off furniture from the garden and bringing on flowerbed to C

Music No. 8B: Scene change

SCENE 5

A secluded corner of the flower garden

There are beds of summer flowers in full bloom, a rose bed and a sundial

Miss Prism and Dr Chasuble enter and break to come down either side of the flowerbed, Miss Prism to LC, Dr Chasuble to RC

Miss Prism You are too much alone, dear Dr Chasuble. You should get
married. (*She moves down*) A misanthrope I can understand—a
womanthrope never!

Dr Chasuble (*with a scholar's shudder*) Believe me, I do not deserve so
neologistic a phrase. The precept as well as the practice of the Primitive
Church was distinctly against matrimony.

Miss Prism That is obviously the reason why the Primitive Church has not
lasted up to the present day. You do not seem to realize, dear Doctor, that
by persistently remaining single, a man converts himself into a permanent
public temptation. (*Looking away from him*)

Dr Chasuble (*moving closer to her below the flowerbed*) I never realized that
a man of the cloth could be a source of temptation, dear lady.

Miss Prism Ah, it all depends on the intellectual sympathies of the woman.
Young women are green. (*Puffing out her chest and turning to face him*)
Ripeness can be trusted.

*Miss Prism moves behind the flowerbed to point at the flowers as Dr Chasuble
breaks to* R

Observe the flowers. Only those in the full maturity of their lifecycle can
convey their true message.

Dr Chasuble Their message, dear lady?

Miss Prism Oh yes, Doctor. Every single flower in the garden carries a
message to the one who receives it.

Music No. 9: Every Flower in the Garden

(*Over the music intro*) The language of the flowers is easy to learn. (*She
moves* DLC)

(*Singing*)   The clover calls, will you be mine,
                     While jasmine is a welcome sign,
                     A bunch of violets say you're shy,
                     The black nightshade means love will die.

Dr Chasuble points to each flower as he sings

Dr Chasuble	The foxglove
Miss Prism	Can bring deep regret.
Dr Chasuble	This daisy
Miss Prism	Vows she won't forget.
Dr Chasuble	The primrose,
Miss Prism	Always brings a sigh.
	The sweet pea bids a fond goodbye.

Chorus
Every flower in the garden
Has a story it can tell
From the hopeful little snowdrop
To the constant sweet bluebell.

Miss Prism crosses to take Dr Chasuble's arm and leads him to LC *of the
flowerbed*

A lover who is turning cold
Will send to you a marigold,
But if she's not quite sure of you
A single primula will do.

Chorus

Miss Prism ⎱ Every flower in the garden
Dr Chasuble ⎰ Has a story it can tell
From the hopeful little snowdrop
To the constant sweet bluebell.

Miss Prism circles up behind the flowerbed to come DR *of it*

Miss Prism   Just see that rose so full and red
It really makes the flowerbed,
And if she gives just one to you
Then you'll know her love is true.

Dr Chasuble realizes he too can use the language of the flowers to say what he feels

Dr Chasuble   I see that rose, it's full and red,
It really makes the flowerbed,
But still it needs the honey bee

Dr Chasuble hands the rose to Miss Prism

To kiss it to maturity.

Miss Prism sighs heavily, Dr Chasuble realizing he may have been too forward adds hurriedly

I was speaking metaphorically.
I state quite categorically
My words were just
Botanically correct.

Miss Prism (*very disappointed and turning away*)
Botanically correct

Dr Chasuble ⎱
Miss Prism ⎰ Every flower in the garden

They meet below the flowerbed; Dr Chasuble takes Miss Prism's hand. Miss Prism is overjoyed to find he does care after all

Has a story it can tell
From the hopeful little snowdrop
To the constant sweet bluebell.

Miss Prism opens her parasol and raises it to hide them as they kiss. They exit

As they do so, the Lights fade and the Servants enter to remove the sundial, flower bed and arbour bushes

SCENE 6

The trellis garden

Music No. 10: Funeral March

After one bar of the music Jack enters slowly. He is dressed in deepest mourning, with crêpe hatband and black gloves. He blows his nose sorrowfully but stops when he finds no-one is watching. He moves to DLC *below the garden bench*

Miss Prism and Dr Chasuble enter and move to DRC *below the garden table and chairs*

Immediately he sees them enter Jack takes out a large handkerchief with a black border and puts it to his eyes

Miss Prism Mr Worthing!
Dr Chasuble Mr Worthing?
Miss Prism This is indeed a surprise. We did not expect you till Monday afternoon.
Jack (*crossing to Dr Chasuble, shaking his hand sadly and speaking in a sombre tone*) I have returned sooner than I expected. Dr Chasuble, I hope you are well?
Dr Chasuble Dear Mr Worthing, I trust this garb of woe does not betoken some terrible calamity?
Jack My brother.
Miss Prism More shameful debts and extravagance?
Dr Chasuble Still leading his life of pleasure?
Jack (*shaking his head*) Dead! (*He dabs his eyes again*)
Dr Chasuble Your brother is dead?
Jack Quite dead. (*Moving away to* L)
Miss Prism What a lesson for him! I trust he will profit by it. (*She sits in the chair* R *of the table*)
Jack (*crossing back in towards* C *with more handkerchief business*) Poor Ernest! He had many faults, but it is a sad, sad blow.
Dr Chasuble Very sad indeed. Were you with him at the end?
Jack No. He died abroad; in Paris, in fact, of a severe chill. I had a telegram last night from the manager of the *Grand Hotel.*
Dr Chasuble Will the internment take place here?
Jack No. He seems to have expressed a desire to be buried in Paris. (*Moving away to* LC)
Dr Chasuble In Paris! (*He shakes his head*) I fear that hardly points to a serious state of mind at the last.
Jack (*suddenly changing his tone to his normal manner*) Ah, that reminds me! Dr Chasuble? I suppose you know how to christen people?

Dr Chasuble looks astounded

Dr Chasuble (*moving to Jack*) Is there any particular infant in whom you are interested, Mr Worthing?

Jack It is not for any child, Doctor. The fact is, I would like to be christened myself, this afternoon, if you have nothing better to do.

Dr Chasuble But surely, Mr Worthing, you have been christened already?

Jack I don't remember anything about it. Of course, if you think I am a little too old now.

Dr Chasuble Not at all. The sprinkling and indeed the immersion of adults is a perfectly canonical practice.

Jack (*with a shudder*) Immersion!

Dr Chasuble Sprinkling is all that is necessary. At what hour would you wish the ceremony to be performed?

Jack (*moving to below the* L *end of the bench*) Oh, I might trot round about five, if that would suit you.

Dr Chasuble Perfectly, perfectly!

Cecily enters as . . .

Dr Chasuble breaks away R *to Miss Prism*

Cecily Uncle Jack! Oh I am pleased to see you back. But what horrid clothes you have got on. Do go and change them.

Miss Prism (*rising*) Cecily!

Dr Chasuble My child! My child!

Cecily goes towards Jack. He kisses her brow in a melancholy manner

Cecily What is the matter, Uncle Jack?

Jack turns away looking grief-stricken

You look as if you have a toothache, and I have got such a surprise for you. Who do you think is in the dining-room? Your brother!

Jack (*startled*) Who?

Cecily Your brother Ernest. He arrived about half an hour ago.

Jack What nonsense! I haven't got a brother. (*Then with deep sadness, remembering his role*) Now.

Cecily Oh, don't say that. However badly he may have behaved to you in the past, he is still your brother. I'll tell him to come out. And you will shake hands with him, won't you, Uncle Jack?

She runs back into the house

Dr Chasuble These are very joyful tidings.

Algernon and Cecily enter hand in hand; Algernon moves to C, *Cecily to the top end of the bench*

Jack Good heavens! (*He glares at Algernon*)

Algernon (*taking no notice*) Brother John, I have come down from town to tell you that I am very sorry for all the trouble I have given you, and that I intend to lead a better life in the future.

He offers his hand to Jack, who turns away

Cecily Uncle Jack, you are not going to refuse your own brother's hand?

Jack Nothing will induce me to take his hand. I think his coming down here is disgraceful. He knows perfectly well why.

Cecily Uncle Jack, do be nice. There is some good in everyone. (*She crosses to Algernon*) Ernest has just been telling me about his poor invalid friend Mr Bunbury whom he goes to visit so often.

Jack eases Cecily away from Algernon, taking her place facing Algernon

Jack Bunbury! I won't have him talking to you about Bunbury or anything else.

Algernon Of course, I admit that the faults were all on my side. But I must say that Brother John's coldness to me is particularly painful.

Cecily (*pulling Jack towards her*) Uncle Jack, if you don't shake hands with Ernest I will never forgive you.

Jack Never forgive me?

Cecily Never!

Jack Very well. But this is the last time I shall ever do it. (*He shakes hands with Algernon and glares at him*)

Dr Chasuble How pleasant to see so perfect a reconciliation. I think we might leave the two brothers together.

Miss Prism Cecily, you will come with us.

Cecily Certainly, Miss Prism.

Miss Prism, Cecily and Dr Chasuble exit

Jack and Algernon continue shaking hands until the others are off then Jack throws Algernon's hand away

Jack I don't want you here, Algy. You've got to go. I'm telling Merriman to get the dogcart for you. (*Calling*) Merriman!

Jack exits L

Algernon starts to follow him but stops when ...

Cecily returns and places her diary and a box of letters on the table

Cecily Oh, I thought Uncle Jack was with you.

Algernon (*moving to Cecily at the table*) He's gone to order the dogcart for me.

Cecily Is he going to take you for a nice drive?

Algernon He's sending me away.

Merriman enters

Merriman I am fetching the dogcart, sir.

Algernon looks appealingly at Cecily

Cecily It can wait, Merriman ... for five minutes.

Merriman Yes, miss.

Merriman exits

Algernon (*breaking away slightly to L*) I hope, Cecily, I shall not offend you if I state quite frankly and openly that you seem to me to be in every way the visible personification of absolute perfection.

Cecily I think your frankness does you great credit, Ernest. If you will allow me, I will copy your remarks into my diary. (*She goes back to the table, sits down, and begins to write*)

Algernon (*moving to the table*) Do you really keep a diary?

Music No. 11: The Importance of Being Ernest

Cecily   It's just a young girl's first reflections
                              On her hopes her dreams and her tears.
Algernon   Please let me see it,
                              Oh do let me read it.

Cecily shields her diary from Algernon

Cecily   Oh no that could never be,
                              But do keep dictating
                              My diary is waiting
                              You stopped at perfection I see.

(*Speaking*) You can go on. I am quite ready for more.

Algernon (*somewhat taken aback and moving away to* C) Ahem! Ahem!

Cecily Oh don't cough, Ernest. When one is dictating one should speak fluently and not cough. Besides, I don't know how to spell a cough.

Cecily writes as Algernon sings

Algernon   I never thought I'd see such beauty
                              So perfect so splendid so fine.

Merriman enters

Merriman The dogcart is waiting, sir.

Algernon Tell it to come round next week at the same hour.

Merriman looks at Cecily who makes no sign

Merriman Yes, sir.
Algernon And Merriman . . .
Merriman Yes, sir.
Algernon You can bring my luggage in.
Merriman Yes, sir.

Merriman exits

Cecily You had reached "splendid and fine".

Algernon moves to the table and kneels

Algernon (*singing*)   I love you so deeply,
                             Wildly completely,
                             Profoundly and quite desperately.
                             Darling, I implore you,
                             I simply adore you,
                             Cecily, please do marry me.

Cecily rises and moves DC, *Algernon gets up and follows her*

Cecily You silly boy! Of course I will. We have been engaged for the last three months.

Algernon For the last three months?

Cecily Yes, it will be exactly three months on Thursday.

Algernon But how did we become engaged?

Cecily Ever since Uncle Jack first confessed to us that he had a younger brother who was very wicked and bad you have been the chief topic of conversation. I dare say it was foolish of me, but I fell in love with you, Ernest.

Algernon Darling. And when was the engagement actually settled?

Cecily On the fourteenth of April last. Worn out by your entire ignorance of my existence, I determined to end the matter one way or the other, and after a long struggle with myself I accepted you. The next day I bought this little ring, and this is the little bangle with the true lover's knot I promised you always to wear. (*She shows it to him*)

Algernon Did I give you this? It's very pretty, isn't it?

Cecily Yes, you have wonderfully good taste, Ernest. It's the excuse I've always given for your leading such a bad life.

Cecily moves to the table and Algernon follows to her L. She picks up the box from the table

And this is the box in which I keep all your dear letters. (*She opens the box and produces the letters tied up with blue ribbon*)

Algernon My letters! But I have never written you any letters.

Cecily You need hardly remind me of that, Ernest. I remember only too well that I was forced to write your letters for you. I wrote always three times a week and sometimes more, but I shall always treasure the first one. (*She sits and takes a letter out of the box*)

Music No. 12: Sincerely Yours

(*Singing*)   You sent a note,
                        A line or two,
                        And all you said
                        Was I love you.
                        Sincerely yours,
                        Sincerely yours.

Cecily rises to Algernon

                        Then I replied
                        A bit too fast
                        I'd found my love,
                        My love at last
                        Sincerely yours,
                        Sincerely yours.

Cecily crosses Algernon to move downstage L. Algernon follows her

                        You wrote so sweetly

> I fell completely
> What could I do
> So now I'll never
> Oh no I'll never
> Stay away from you.

She moves to Algernon who takes her right hand

> How could I know
> How soft your touch
> Or how two words
> Could mean so much?
> Sincerely yours,
> Sincerely yours.

Algernon (*speaking*) Do let me read my letters, Cecily.

Cecily removes her hand and goes to the table to return the letter to the box. Algernon follows

Cecily Oh I couldn't possibly. They would make you far too conceited. The three you wrote me after I had broken off the engagement are so beautiful, and so badly spelled, that even now I can hardly read them without crying a little.

Algernon But was our engagement ever broken off?

Cecily Of course it was. On the twenty-second of last May. You can see the entry if you like. (*She picks up her diary and shows it to him*) "Today I broke off my engagement with Ernest. I feel it is better to do so. The weather still continues charming." (*She sits in a chair*)

Algernon But why on earth did you break it off?

Cecily It would hardly have been a really serious engagement if it hadn't been broken off at least once. But I forgave you before the week was out.

Algernon kneels

> (*Singing*)   You wrote so sweetly
> I fell completely,
> What could I do?
> So now I'll never,
> Oh no, I'll never
> Stay away from you.

> How could I know
> How soft your touch
> Or how two words
> Could mean so much?
> Sincerely yours,
> Sincerely yours.

Algernon (*kissing her hand*) What a perfect angel you are, Cecily.

Cecily You dear romantic boy.

Algernon We must never part again.

Cecily We never shall, Ernest. (*She looks at her watch*) But I see the time is just before three o'clock and my dress rehearsal for the tableau is due to start on the hour. I must leave you.

Cecily rises and crosses Algernon to C. *Algernon gets up and follows her*

Algernon Considering that we have been engaged since April the fourteenth and that I only met you today for the first time, I think it is rather hard that you should leave so quickly. When will I see you again?
Cecily For tea, at three-thirty precisely.

Cecily exits

Jack enters and confronts Algernon below the table

Jack What are you still doing here, Algy? I told you before I want you to go.

Merriman enters to C

Merriman I am putting Mr Ernest's luggage in the room next to yours, sir.
Jack His luggage?

Music No. 13: Your Duty as a Gentleman

Servants enter in a line carrying Algernon's luggage

Jack circles below the Servants to L *of them. The Servants end up in a diagonal line holding luggage. Merriman joins at the* L *end, then crosses in front of them to join them at the* R *end*

Servants   A dressing case that wouldn't disgrace
          A bishop's wardrobe, oh your grace!
          A luncheon basket and a stick
          With a gold-topped end that goes click click
          And hats and boxes and riding togs
          And a portmanteau like a French château.

Jack moves to inspect the cases then turns angrily to Algernon below the line of Servants

Jack (*speaking*) I want to make it clear there'll be no Bunburying here. (*He moves away to* L *and then turns to advance on Algernon*)

          Your presence here is quite disgraceful
          In fact you've got an awful cheek
          And bringing all this luggage with you
          You've got enough to stay the week.

Jack advances again on Algernon

          I don't care where you Bunbury
          As long as it isn't here.

Jack moves away to LC. *Algernon follows*

Algernon   But this time, my dear dear brother,
                  My intentions are quite sincere.

Jack advances again on Algernon who retreats from Jack's pointing finger

Jack   Your duty as a gentleman
                  Calls you back to town
                  So, Merriman, fetch the dogcart
                  And put that luggage down.

This last to the Servants holding the luggage

*Merriman and the Servants place all the items back in a pile C, as Jack moves
away to LC, followed by Algernon*

Algernon   Your attitude is most unfriendly,
                  I've never been in love before.
Jack   Why almost every week you tell me
                  There's some new girl you just adore.

Algernon moves to R of the pile of luggage

Algernon   No morbid undertaker (*pointing at Jack*)
                  Dressed up like a big black crow
                  Is going to give me orders.

*Jack comes to L of the luggage, picks up a hatbox and throws it at Algernon as
he sings "go"*

Jack   I tell you that you've got to go.
Algernon   No duty as a gentleman
                  Calls me, my dear Jack.
                  So, Merriman, leave the dogcart

Algernon throws back to the hatbox to Jack on the word "back"

                  And take my luggage back.

*Jack catches the hatbox and immediately throws it over his head where it is
caught by a Servant. The other Servants pick up the luggage and stand in line*

Jack   Your vanity is quite ridiculous.
Algernon   You're pompous and you're just absurd.
Jack   And if you stay a moment longer
                  I'm going to say a very rude word.
Algernon   Bah!

Jack ushers Algernon towards the exit R

Jack   You're going to the station
                  And catching the ten past four
                  So enjoy a pleasant journey.
Algernon   You'll never get me through that door.

Jack advances on the lingering Algernon

Jack   Your duty as a gentleman
                    Calls you back to town,
                    So, Merriman, fetch the dogcart
                    And take that luggage out.

Jack leads the Servants off R *in a line; then re-appears alone to pull Algernon off with him*

The Lights fade to Black-out as——

                    —the CURTAIN *falls*

ACT II

Music No. 14: Entr'acte

SCENE 1

The topiary garden

There are two garden benches L *and* R. *The Servants are creating their full dress rehearsal for Cecily's Empire League Tableau. Merriman and another Servant are holding large Union Jack and Empire flags over the seated Queen Victoria, flanked by Florence Nightingale and Britannia. Behind them are John Bull, Nelson and Disraeli and maids with smaller flags. Cecily is standing* DL *of the group*

Cecily (*moving in to below the* L *bench*) That was a truly patriotic display.

The Servants relax their poses as she starts to speak

The Queen would be very proud of you, Mrs Broom. You must wear an eye patch on Saturday, Harold, Lord Nelson would never have been seen in public without it.

Algernon enters to below the R *bench*

Algernon Cecily.
Cecily (*crossing to Algernon*) Ernest! What are you doing here?
Algernon I couldn't wait until tea to see you again.
Cecily One must never be impatient, Ernest.

Algernon approaches Cecily who breaks away to below the L *bench*

Algernon I will always be impatient to see you, my darling.
Cecily I must finish my rehearsal, Ernest. (*To the Servants*) I want you all to remember to wear your best shoes and boots on Saturday.
Servants ⎫
Merriman ⎭ (*together*) Yes, miss. Thank you, miss.
Cecily That will be all, Merriman.

The Servants exit taking Queen Victoria's chair with them and all their props, except Nelson's hat which is left on the bench R, *where two swords in sheaths are already present for later use*

Algernon and Cecily meet

Algernon Promise me you'll never break off our engagement again.

Cecily I don't think I could ever break it off now that I've actually met you. Besides there is the question of your name.

Algernon Yes, of course.

Cecily You must not laugh at me, darling, but it had always been a girlish dream of mine to love someone whose name was Ernest. There is something in that name that seems to inspire absolute confidence. I pity any poor married woman whose husband is not called Ernest.

Algernon But my dear angel, do you mean to say you could not love me if I had some other name?

Cecily (*turning to face him*) What other name?

Algernon Oh any other name—Algernon—for instance ...

Algernon follows Cecily as she moves to LC

Cecily But I don't like Algernon.

Algernon (*following her*) I can't see why you object to Algernon. It's rather an aristocratic name. Half the fellows in the Bankruptcy Court and the Army are called Algernon. Seriously. Cecily, if my name was Algernon ... couldn't you love me?

Music No. 15: The Importance of Being Ernest

Cecily crosses to the bench R

Cecily   Algernon, Algernon, it may sound fine
In a bankruptcy court or review.
No I assure you, my dearest,
That's one name that would never ever do.

Cecily returns to face Algernon

The importance of being Ernest
Is something that will never change.

Algernon (*speaking*) But my darling——
Cecily (*singing*)   In all creation,

She pushes him down on to the bench

The whole British nation
No-one but Ernest will do.

Algernon (*speaking*) But Cecily——
Cecily (*singing*)   So kindly remember
I'll never surrender
To anyone else but you.

Algernon (*rising to Cecily, speaking*) But there are lots of wonderful names.

Cecily crosses Algernon to the bench L *and sits*

Cecily (*singing*)   The one name in this world
That is quite perfect to me,
The one name in this world
That is quite perfect to me.

> The importance of being Ernest
> Is something I'll never forget.
> Your name is divine
> And it goes well with mine,
> It sounds so honest and free,
> I'll never discover
> True love with another
> I've made up my mind you see.

Algernon (*moving to Cecily, speaking*) Ahem! Cecily! Your rector here is, I suppose, thoroughly experienced in the practice of all the rites and ceremonies of the Church?

Cecily Oh yes. Dr Chasuble is a most learned man.

Algernon I must see him at once on a most important christening—I mean on most important business.

Cecily Oh!

Algernon I'll be back in no time.

Algernon kisses her and exits

Cecily What an impetuous boy he is. I must enter his proposal in my diary. (*She picks up her diary which is on the bench* L)

Merriman enters and moves to the bench L

Merriman A Miss Fairfax has just called to see Mr Worthing, on very important business, Miss Fairfax states.

Cecily Isn't Mr Worthing in the library?

Merriman Mr Worthing went over in the direction of the Rectory some time ago.

Cecily Ask the lady to come in here. And you can bring tea.

Merriman Yes, miss.

He exits

Cecily Miss Fairfax! She must be one of the many good elderly women who are associated with Uncle Jack in his philanthropic work in London.

Merriman enters

Merriman Miss Fairfax.

Gwendolen enters and moves to below the bench R

Merriman retires

Cecily (*rising and advancing to meet her* C) Let me introduce myself. My name is Cecily Cardew.

Gwendolen Cecily Cardew? (*Moving to her and shaking her hand*) What a very sweet name!

Cecily Pray sit down. (*She moves back to the bench* L)

Gwendolen (*still standing up*) I may call you Cecily, may I not?

Cecily With pleasure!

Gwendolen And you will always call me Gwendolen, won't you?

Cecily If you wish.

Music No. 16: I Am Never Wrong

Gwendolen I am already quite fond of you, Cecily. In fact . . .

(*Singing*)   The moment I saw you I knew we'd be friends
                And when I form a friendship it really never ends.
                I feel we are sisters though I haven't known you long

Gwendolen moves to C

                And I am never wrong, my dear, I am never wrong.
                Our secrets we'll share and every problem too
                Though fate may divide us my thoughts will stay with you.
                I'm glad that I've met you for I know we belong
                And I am never wrong, my dear, I am never wrong.

Cecily   How nice of you to like me and to say such charming things
                I never cease to marvel at the good things each day brings.
                If we have so much in common it cannot be ignored,
                This is a happy moment which I really must record.

Cecily returns L *to sit with her diary*

Gwendolen   No promise was given when you took my hand

Gwendolen moves downstairs RC

                But you can still trust me to help and understand
                I know my affection will be steadfast and strong
                And I am never wrong, my dear, I am never wrong.

Cecily (*rising*) To make a friend after such a comparatively short time is
truly gratifying. Pray do sit down.

They both sit down, Cecily on the bench L, *Gwendolen on the bench* R. *There is
a pause; they look at each other and smile, then look out front again*

Gwendolen Perhaps this might be a favourable opportunity to mention who
I am. My father is Lord Bracknell. You have never heard of Papa I
suppose?

Cecily I don't think so.

Gwendolen Outside the family circle, Papa, I am glad to say, is entirely
unknown. I think that is quite as it should be. Mamma, whose views on
education are remarkably strict, has brought me up to be extremely short
sighted; it is part of her system; so do you mind my looking at you more
closely through my glasses?

Cecily rises while Gwendolen inspects her through her lorgnette

Cecily Oh, not at all, Gwendolen. I am very fond of being looked at.

Gwendolen You are here on a short visit, I suppose?

Cecily Oh no! I live here.

Gwendolen (*severely*) Really? Your mother, no doubt, or some female
relative of advanced years, resides here also?

Cecily Oh no! I have no mother, nor, in fact, any relations.

Gwendolen Indeed?

Cecily My dear guardian, with the assistance of Miss Prism, has the arduous task of looking after me.

Gwendolen Your guardian?

Cecily Yes, I am Mr Worthing's ward.

Gwendolen It is strange he never mentioned to me that he had a ward. How secretive of him! He grows more interesting hourly. I am not sure, however, that the news inspires me with feelings of unmixed delight. In fact, if I may be candid . . .

Cecily Pray do! (*Moving back to the bench*) I think that whenever one has anything unpleasant to say, one should always be quite candid.

Gwendolen (*rising*) Well, to speak with perfect candour, Cecily, I wish that you were fully forty-two, and more than unusually plain for your age. Ernest is the very soul of truth and honour. But even men of the noblest possible moral character are susceptible to the physical charms of others.

Cecily (*moving* C) I beg your pardon, Gwendolen, did you say Ernest?

Gwendolen Yes.

Cecily Oh, but it is not Mr Ernest Worthing who is my guardian. It is his brother—his eldest brother.

Gwendolen Ernest never mentioned to me that he had a brother.

Cecily I am sorry to say they have not been on good terms for a long time.

Gwendolen Ah, that accounts for it. (*Crossing to take Cecily's hand*) Cecily, you have lifted a load from my mind. I was growing almost anxious. It would have been terrible if any cloud had come across a friendship like ours, would it not? (*She lets go of Cecily's hand and turns away*) Of course you are quite, quite sure that it is not Mr Ernest Worthing who is your guardian?

Cecily Quite sure. (*After a slight pause*) In fact, I am going to be his.

Gwendolen (*enquiringly*) I beg your pardon?

Cecily (*confiding*) Dearest Gwendolen, there is no reason why I should make a secret of it to you. Our little county newspaper is sure to chronicle the fact next week. Mr Ernest Worthing and I are engaged to be married.

Gwendolen (*very politely*) My darling Cecily, I think there must be some slight error. Mr Ernest Worthing is engaged to me. The announcement will appear in the *Morning Post* on Saturday at the latest.

Cecily (*very politely*) I am afraid you must be under some misconception. Ernest proposed to me exactly five minutes ago. (*She crosses to pick up her diary and shows it to Gwendolen*)

Gwendolen (*examining the diary carefully*) It is certainly very curious for he asked me to be his wife yesterday afternoon at five-thirty. If you would care to verify the incident, pray do so. I never travel without my diary. One should always have something sensational to read on the train. (*She produces a diary of her own which she hands to Cecily*) I am so sorry, dear Cecily, if it is any disappointment to you, but I am afraid I have the prior claim.

Cecily It would distress me more than I can tell you, dear Gwendolen, if it caused you any mental or physical anguish but I feel bound to point out that since Ernest proposed to you he has clearly changed his mind.

Cecily and Gwendolen return diaries to each other and move to the benches L *and* R *respectively*

Gwendolen (*firmly*) If the poor fellow has been entrapped into any foolish promise I shall consider it my duty to rescue him at once, and with a firm hand.

Gwendolen and Cecily face away from each other

Cecily (*thoughtfully and sadly*) Whatever unfortunate entanglement my dear boy may have got into, I will never reproach him with it after we are married.

They turn to face each other

Gwendolen Do you allude to me, Miss Cardew, as an entanglement? You are presumptuous. On an occasion of this kind it becomes more than a moral duty to speak one's mind—it becomes a pleasure.

Cecily Do you suggest, Miss Fairfax, that I entrapped Ernest into an engagement? How dare you? This is no time for wearing the shallow mask of manners. When I see a spade I call it a spade.

Gwendolen I'm glad to say that I have never seen a spade.

Merriman enters

Merriman Shall I lay for tea, miss?

Cecily (*sternly, in a calm voice*) Yes, we will have it now, Merriman.

Merriman Very good, miss. (*He motions to the Servants*)

The Servants bring in the tea trolleys

Gwendolen and Cecily move away DL *and* DR *while tea is laid*

SCENE 2

The Terrace

Music No. 17: May I Offer You a Cup of Tea?

Cecily and Gwendolen remain DL *and* DR *as ...*

Two Manservants enter with a garden table which they set C, *while two others move the benches away to either side. Merriman and Mrs Broom wheel the two tea trolleys to* UL. *Four Maids enter and stand ready to take cups, saucers etc. to the tea table. They always move in time with the music*

Two maids Annie and Jane collect a table-cloth from the trolley. They move to the table and divide either side of it each taking one end of the cloth in their hands. They stretch it out and place it on the table in one movement and return to the trolley

Two maids, Alice and Mabel collect a lace overlay. They divide either side of the table each taking one end of the overlay, stretch it out and place it on the table in one movement. They return to the trolley

Annie and Jane collect milk, sugar, tea-strainer and sugar-tongs from the trolley. They place them on the table and return to the trolley

Alice and Mabel collect plates, cups and saucers from the trolley. They place them on the table and return to the trolley

Annie and Jane collect spoons, knives and cake forks from the trolley. They place them on the table and return to the trolley

Jane exits

Alice collects bread and muffins from the trolley. She places them on the table and returns to the trolley. Mabel collects jam and honey from the trolley. She places them on the table and returns to the trolley. Annie collects a cake from the trolley. She places it on the table and returns to the trolley. Annie collects a cake from the trolley. She places it on the table and returns to the trolley

Jane enters carrying a vase of flowers which she places on the table and moves
UL

Two Manservants bring on two chairs which they place either side of the tea table

Merriman wheels the tea trolley to above the tea table and places the teapot on the table. All Servants stand in a line US. *Cecily sits* L *of the table*

Cecily (*singing*) I hope that you will sit here next to me
                And may I offer you a cup of tea?

Cecily pours tea

Gwendolen   (*aside*) How can she be so sweet,
                That smile is pure deceit.
Cecily   One or two lumps for you?

Gwendolen sits in the chair R *of the tea table and observes the garden*

Gwendolen   None for me—not in tea.

Cecily puts several lumps into the cup

Cecily   Da da dee da da dee
                Just a few—that should do.

She empties the sugar bowl into the cup and hands the cup to a Maid who keeps in time with the music as she carries it to Gwendolen

Gwendolen   (*still looking at the garden*)
                Your garden must be quite as big as ours
                I am surprised to see so many flowers.
Cecily   (*very sweetly*) Oh they're as common here
                As people in your sphere.

Cecily picks up a plate

                Will you take bread or cake?
Gwendolen   (*still admiring the garden*)   .
                Bread is nice—just one slice.

Cecily cuts a large slice of cake and puts the remainder on a plate

Cecily   Da da dee da da dee
          (*To a Maid*) Where's the mat? Give her that.

Cecily hands the plate to a Maid who places it on a mat on her tray and takes it to Gwendolen who reacts strongly when she finds she has tea with sugar and cake instead of bread. The Servants all turn their backs as Gwendolen rises. She is obviously angry

Gwendolen   You start by being so polite and offer me some tea
          But when I say I want no sugar you fill a cup for me.
          I know I said I wanted bread but all I get is cake.
          If you are testing my restraint you've made a big mistake.

Gwendolen sits again. Cecily rises as she gives her reply

Cecily   To save my boy from being led astray
          I'd fight a thousand dragons every day.

She suddenly changes her tone to one of utter reasonableness

          And now I've made that clear

She sits; even more sweetly

          More tea for you, my dear?

Both are now speaking with restrained anger

          One or two lumps for you?
Gwendolen   Not for me—not in tea.
Cecily   Da da dee da da dee

The Servants turn to face front. Merriman puts a second teapot on the table and indicates to the Servants to go off

  The Servants all exit, wheeling off the tea trolleys

Cecily and Gwendolen remain silent until the Servants have left

Gwendolen   (*rising*)
          The moment I saw you I knew you were false
          You'd tell a man you love him then dance a crooked waltz.

Cecily rises

          I knew you were deceitful and your friendship wasn't strong
          And I am *never* wrong, my dear, I am *never* wrong.
          No I am never wrong, my dear, I am never wrong.

They separate. Cecily moves L, *Gwendolen* R

  Jack enters R

Gwendolen (*catching sight of him*) Ernest! My own Ernest!

Jack (*advancing to her*) Gwendolen! Darling! (*He offers to kiss her*)
Gwendolen (*drawing back*) One moment! May I ask if you are engaged to be married to this young lady? (*She points to Cecily*)
Jack (*laughing*) To dear little Cecily! Of course not! What could have put such an idea into your pretty little head?
Gwendolen Thank you. You may! (*She offers her cheek*)

Jack kisses her

Cecily (*very sweetly, moving towards the table*) I knew there must be some misunderstanding, Miss Fairfax. The gentleman whose arm is at present round your waist is my guardian, Mr John Worthing.
Gwendolen I beg your pardon?
Cecily This is Uncle Jack.
Gwendolen (*receding*) Jack!

Algernon enters

Cecily Here is Ernest.

Algernon goes straight over to Cecily at L of the table without acknowledging Jack or anyone else and tries to embrace her

Algernon My own darling!
Cecily (*drawing back*) A moment, Ernest! May I ask you—are you engaged to be married to this young lady?
Algernon (*looking round*) To what young lady? Good heavens! Gwendolen!
Cecily Yes! To good heavens Gwendolen—I mean to Gwendolen.
Algernon (*laughing*) Of course not! What could have put such an idea into your pretty little head?
Cecily Thank you. (*She presents her cheek to be kissed*) You may.

Algernon kisses her

Gwendolen I felt there was some slight error, Miss Cardew. The gentleman who is now embracing you is my cousin, Mr Algernon Moncrieff . . .
Cecily (*breaking away from Algernon*) Algernon Moncrieff! (*To Algernon*) Are you called Algernon?
Algernon I cannot deny it.
Cecily Oh!
Gwendolen Is your name really Jack?
Jack (*standing rather proudly*) I could deny it if I liked. But my name is Jack. It has been Jack for years.
Cecily (*to Gwendolen*) A gross deception has been practised on both of us.

Gwendolen crosses Jack to below the tea table

Gwendolen My poor wounded Cecily!

Cecily crosses Algernon to below the tea table to meet Gwendolen

Cecily My sweet wronged Gwendolen!

Cecily and Gwendolen exchange kisses. Jack and Algernon groan and turn away

But where is Ernest?

Gwendolen Yes, Mr Worthing, where is your brother Ernest? We are both engaged to be married to your brother Ernest, so it is a matter of some importance to us to know where your brother Ernest is at present.

Algernon Yes.

Jack (*slowly and hesitatingly*) Gwendolen—Cecily—it is very painful for me to be forced to speak the truth. However, I will tell you quite frankly that I have no brother Ernest. I have no brother at all.

Cecily (*surprised*) No brother at all?

Jack None!

Gwendolen (*severely*) You have never had a brother of any kind?

Jack Never. Not even of any kind.

Gwendolen I am afraid it is quite clear, Cecily, that neither of us is engaged to be married to anyone. (*To Jack and Algernon*) We wish to discuss our future in private.

Gwendolen crosses to join Cecily in front of the tea table, as Jack and Algernon move respectively to R *and* L

Cecily It is not a very pleasant position for a young girl suddenly to find herself in.

Gwendolen Let us go into the house. (*She takes Cecily away up* C) They will hardly venture to come after us there.

Cecily No, men are so cowardly, aren't they?

Cecily and Gwendolen retire into the house with scornful looks

Algernon sits in the chair L *of the tea table and starts to pour tea and eat the muffins. Jack sits in the chair* R *of the tea table*

Jack This ghastly state of affairs is what you call Bunburying, I suppose.

Algernon Yes, it's the most wonderful Bunbury I have ever had in my life.

Jack The only small satisfaction I have in the whole of this wretched business is that your friend Bunbury is quite exploded. You won't be able to run down to the country quite so often as you used to do, dear Algy. And a very good thing too.

Algernon (*continuing to eat the muffins*) Your brother is a little off-colour too, isn't he, dear Jack? You won't be able to pop up to London quite so frequently.

Jack How can you sit there calmly eating muffins when we are in this horrible trouble? You seem to be perfectly heartless.

Algernon At the present moment I am eating muffins because I am unhappy. Besides, I am particularly fond of muffins.

Jack Well that is no reason why you should eat them all in that greedy way. (*He reaches for a muffin*)

Algernon I wish you would have a tea-cake instead. I don't like tea-cake.

Jack (*rising*) Good heavens! I suppose a man may eat his own muffins in his own garden.

Algernon But you have just said it was perfectly heartless to eat muffins.

Jack I said it was perfectly heartless of you under the circumstances. That is a very different thing.

Algernon That may be. But the muffins are the same.

Jack Algy, I wish to goodness you would go.

Algernon You can't possibly ask me to go without having some dinner. It's absurd. I never go without my dinner. Besides, I've just made an arrangement with Dr Chasuble to be christened at a quarter to six under the name of Ernest.

Jack (*moving* R *towards the bench*) The sooner you give up that nonsense the better. I made arrangements this morning with Dr Chasuble to be christened myself at five-thirty and naturally I will take the name Ernest. Gwendolen would wish it. We can't both be christened Ernest. It's absurd. Besides I have a perfect right to be christened. There is no evidence at all that I have ever been christened by anybody. It is entirely different in your case. You have been christened already.

Algernon Yes, but I haven't been christened for years.

Jack Yes, but you have been christened. That's the important thing.

Algernon Quite so — so I know my constitution can stand it.

Jack That is nonsense. (*He sits on the bench, but finds he's got a sword and Nelson's hat underneath him. He jumps up again*) Ouch! I wish the Empire League would hold their rehearsals in some other garden. (*He throws the sword and the hat on the floor below the tea table*)

Algernon (*picking up the hat and trying it on*) I always fancied myself in uniform — quite smart don't you think?

Jack collects a second sword from the bench R as Algernon picks up the one at his feet. Jack advances menacingly sword in hand towards Algernon who retreats to the L bench

Jack Algernon, I have already told you what to do. I don't want you here. (*He returns to* R *of the tea table*) And as for your conduct towards Miss Cardew, I must say that your taking in a sweet, simple, innocent girl like that is quite inexcusable. To say nothing of the fact that she is my ward.

Algernon advances to L of the tea table, taking off Nelson's hat and putting it on the chair

Algernon I can see no possible defence at all for your deceiving a brilliant, clever, thoroughly experienced young lady like Miss Fairfax. To say nothing of the fact that she is my cousin.

Jack I wanted to be engaged to Gwendolen. I love her.

Algernon Well, I simply wanted to be engaged to Cecily. I adore her.

They stand shoulder to shoulder in front of the tea table glaring at each other

Jack I would do anything for Gwendolen.

Algernon I would do anything for Cecily.

Music No. 18: Yes For a Woman We Will

Jack	Why does a man climb a mountain
	Who never before tried a hill?
Algernon	Not for the view or to please you

But for a woman he will.

Both men break to sides of the tea table

	Orders more top coats and trousers,
Jack	Forgets about paying the bill,
	Wears a cravat that matches her hat——
Algernon	No!
Jack	Yes, for a woman he will.

Jack moves to the front of the tea table

The moment has come when I must say goodbye
To a name that is noble and true.

Algernon moves to the front of the tea table to stand beside Jack

It's a mortal blow but Jack must go,
I know what I have to do.

They separate, unsheathe swords and parry

	Give up my clubs and my drinking
Algernon	No, never!

They lean on the swords as walking sticks

Jack	I know that it's madness, but still,
	It's quite absurd just one little word
	Then for a woman you will.

Four male Servants enter to remove the two chairs and the tea table

	Starts writing verse about lovers
Algernon	Who never before showed the skill.
Jack	No, couldn't write rhymes for *The Tatler*
Algernon	Or *Times*
Jack	But for a woman he will.
Algernon	The moment has come when I must say goodbye
	To a name that is noble and true.
Jack	You're copying me.
Algernon	No Algy must go
	I know what I have to do.

The four Servants line up US behind Jack and Algernon and join in the end of their military march routine

Jack	What man would give up his birthright
Algernon	And do what we have to fulfil?
Jack	Change your first name,
Algernon	And you'd do the same,
Jack	Yes for a woman
Algernon	Yes for a woman
	Yes for a woman

We will
We will.

Jack and Algernon finish their routine with a sword salute and exit while . . .

The Servants re-position the two benches and then go off

Music No. 18A: Play-off music

Music No. 18B: Scene change music

SCENE 3

The conservatory

It is light and airy and a door at the back leads to the garden

Gwendolen and Cecily enter to US. *They are looking* L

Gwendolen The fact that they did not follow us at once, as anyone else
would have done, seems to me to show that they have some sense of
shame left.
Cecily They have been eating muffins. That looks like repentance.
Gwendolen (*after a pause*) They don't seem to notice us at all. Couldn't you
cough?
Cecily But I haven't got a cough.
Gwendolen They're looking at us. What effrontery!
Cecily They're approaching. That's very forward of them.

Cecily and Gwendolen move down to below the bench L, *as . . .*

Algernon and Jack, whistling "Yes, For a Woman We Will", enter L *and
walk down to below the bench* R

Gwendolen Let us preserve a dignified silence.
Cecily Certainly. It is the only thing to do now.

The ladies sit on the L *bench and the men on the* R *bench. After a short pause
Gwendolen rises, moves to* C

Music No. 19: One Vital Question

Gwendolen (*speaking*) Mr Worthing.

Jack rises and moves to join her

(*Singing*)   There is one vital question I would like to ask
Although I do not welcome this most unpleasant task,
Why did you invent a brother, a naughty poppinjay,

Giving him the answer to her question

Unless it was to come to town to see me every day?

To which Jack happily agrees

Jack (*speaking*) Can you doubt it, Miss Fairfax?

Gwendolen addresses Cecily

Gwendolen (*singing*)	The simple beauty of that answer
	I find quite dignified.
	What can a woman do
	When she is faced by someone who
	Is more, yes more than justified?
Cecily	(*pointedly*) You could say no.
Gwendolen	(*agreeing*) Yes that is so
	I could say no,

But that is clearly not what Gwendolen wants to do

But I'd mean yes
Oh I'd mean yes.

Jack and Gwendolen return to their respective seats. Cecily gets up and moves to C

Cecily (*speaking*) Mr Moncrieff.

Algernon rises and moves to join her

(*Singing*)	There is one vital question I would like to ask
	Although I do not welcome this most unpleasant task
	Why did you pretend your brother was my guardian Jack

And then gives him the answer

Unless it was to meet me here behind my uncle's back?

Algernon happily agrees

Algernon (*speaking*) How can you question it, Miss Cardew?

Cecily addresses Gwendolen

Cecily (*singing*)	The simple beauty of that answer
	I find quite dignified
	What can a woman do
	When she is faced by someone who
	Is more, yes more than justified?
Gwendolen	You could say no,
Cecily	Yes that is so
	I could say no

But Cecily also knows what she really wants

But I'd mean yes
Oh I'd mean yes.

Gwendolen rises and comes behind Cecily to her R as Cecily moves DS

Gwendolen	There is one vital statement both of us must make:
Cecily	Your Christian names are wrong our honour is at stake.

Algernon and Jack together move down to the ladies' level

Algernon ⎫
Jack ⎭   If that's the only problem then we'll solve it very soon

Jack and Algernon put their arms around each other's shoulders

In fact we're both being christened here this very afternoon.

They drop their arms

Gwendolen ⎫
Cecily ⎭   The simple beauty of that answer
We find quite dignified
What can a woman do
When she is faced by someone who
Is more, yes more than justified?

Gwendolen	(*pointing out*) We could say no
Cecily	(*agreeing*) Yes that is so

Gwendolen ⎫
Cecily ⎭   We could say no

Cecily meets Algernon LC *as he moves to her and Gwendolen crosses Algernon to join Jack. The couples hold hands and kiss*

But we'd mean yes
Oh we'd mean yes (*half-spoken*)
Oh we'd mean yes.

Gwendolen (*speaking*) Darling!
Jack Darling!

They embrace

Cecily Darling!
Algernon Darling!

They embrace

Music No. 19A: One Love Dance

The couples waltz to the music as . . .

The Servants enter to remove the benches and set the furniture for the next scene, then exit

SCENE 4

The library of the Manor House, Woolton

It is a large and imposing room which leads directly on to the conservatory. Beyond we can see the trees and flowers of the garden. The room is tastefully and elegantly decorated and furnished. There is either a series of bookshelves on one wall or a small revolving bookcase on one side containing a large selection of leather-backed books

We hear a commotion outside the door. Merriman enters and coughs when he sees the couples together

Merriman Ahem, ahem. Lady Bracknell.

Lady Bracknell enters dressed in suitable clothes for travelling in a first-class compartment of the London Midland and Scottish Railway

Jack Good heavens!

The couples separate in alarm

Merriman exits

Lady Bracknell moves c with Jack, Gwendolen, Cecily and Algernon on her L below the table and chairs

Lady Bracknell Gwendolen! What does this mean?

Gwendolen Merely that I am engaged to be married to Mr Worthing, Mamma.

Lady Bracknell Come here. Sit down immediately. (*She points to the settee*)

Gwendolen sits at the DS end of the settee

(*To Jack*) Appraised, sir, of my daughter's sudden flight by her trusty maid, whose confidences I purchased by means of a small coin, I followed her at once by a luggage train. You will clearly understand that all communication between yourself and my daughter must cease immediately. On this point, as indeed on all points, I am firm.

Jack I am engaged to be married to Gwendolen, Lady Bracknell!

Lady Bracknell You are nothing of the kind, sir. (*She sits on the settee above Gwendolen*) And now, as regards Algernon ... Algernon!

Algernon Yes, Aunt Augusta?

Algernon moves forward with Cecily as Jack moves to below the table

Lady Bracknell May I ask if it is in this house that your invalid friend Mr Bunbury resides?

Algernon (*startled*) Oh no! Bunbury doesn't live here. Bunbury is somewhere else at present. In fact Bunbury is dead.

Lady Bracknell Dead! When did Mr Bunbury die? His death must have been extremely sudden.

Algernon (*airily*) Oh! I killed Bunbury this afternoon. I mean poor Bunbury died this afternoon.

Lady Bracknell What did he die of?

Algernon Bunbury? Oh, he was quite exploded.

Lady Bracknell Exploded! Was he the victim of some revolutionary outrage?

Algernon He was found out! The doctors found out that Bunbury could not live, that is what I mean—so Bunbury died. (*He takes hold of Cecily's hand*)

Lady Bracknell He seems to have had great confidence in the opinion of his physicians. However I am glad that he made up his mind at last to take some definite course of action and acted under proper medical advice. And now that we have finally got rid of Mr Bunbury, may I ask, Mr Worthing, who is that young person whose hand my nephew Algernon is now holding in what seems to me a peculiarly unnecessary manner?

Jack That lady is Miss Cecily Cardew, my ward.

Jack takes Cecily to be introduced to Lady Bracknell, as Algernon moves to below the table

Algernon Miss Cardew and I are engaged to be married, Aunt Augusta.

Lady Bracknell I beg your pardon?

Cecily Mr Moncrieff and I are engaged to be married, Lady Bracknell. (*She crosses Jack to Algernon's* L)

Lady Bracknell (*with a shiver*) I do not know whether there is anything peculiarly exciting in the air of this particular part of Hertfordshire, but the number of engagements that go on seems to me considerably above the proper average that statistics have laid down for our guidance. I think that under the circumstances some preliminary enquiry on my part would not be out of place.

Music No. 20: My Ward/Your Engagement

Lady Bracknell rises to Jack

(*Singing*)   There are certain considerations
When it comes to choosing a bride.
Does Miss Cardew have any parents
Or should I refer to the *Railway Guide*?

Jack (*annoyed by Lady Bracknell's words, leading Cecily away to* LC)
My ward is descended from the Cardews of Ware
With houses in York, Bath and Berkeley Square.
I trust three addresses are better than one.

Lady Bracknell (*condescendingly as she moves* DRC)
They might impress the tradesmen when business is done.

Jack (*even more annoyed by this reply*)
Her family advisors are Markbys of the Lane.

Lady Bracknell Markby, Markby and Markby you mean?

Jack   The same,

Jack moves C *towards Lady Bracknell*

So at least their advice can't have been bad.

Lady Bracknell Depending of course on which Markby they had.

Algernon remains by the chair at R *of the table. Jack rejoins Cecily below the table*

Jack   I have in my possession her certificates of birth,
                    Of whooping cough and measles and everything on earth.
                    If there is any document you would like to see?
Lady Bracknell I think I've already heard too much variety.

(*Speaking*) It's not good for a young girl you know. (*She looks at her watch and turns to leave*) Gwendolen, the time approaches for our departure. Come my dear, or we will miss our train.

Gwendolen rises to go but Lady Bracknell pauses and then turns to Jack

(*Singing*)   Just as a matter of form I ought to verify
                  Whether Miss Cardew has any any little fortune put by.
(*She turns to leave. She is so convinced that Miss Cardew will have no fortune that she has already taken two steps towards the door* US *when she hears the sum of money in Miss Cardew's fortune*)
Jack   Just a hundred and thirty thousand pounds or so.
                  Goodbye Lady Bracknell, so sorry you have to go.

She stops and then slowly turns with a look of great interest on her face as she examines Cecily properly for the first time

Lady Bracknell A hundred and thirty thousand pounds did you say?

She raises her lorgnette and examines Cecily carefully for the first time. Gwendolen sits down again on the settee

                  Now I see Miss Cardew I think I should stay.

She sits down again on the settee next to Gwendolen

                  She seems most attractive and will improve with time,
                  I feel she has values rather like mine.

She beckons Cecily who moves closer

                  I must see you closer, let me look at your clothes.
                  That dress is quite charming but no-one wears those.
                  (*Indicating a brooch on Cecily's dress*)
                  The hair is too natural and the curls are too tight
                  But I know a French maid who'll soon put it right.

Lady Bracknell rises to Cecily

                  My child, your engagement will be
                  Considered by me very carefully.
                  My child, your profile is fine,
                  But do keep the back and chin both in line.

                  My nephew has nothing no houses or carriages
                  But I don't approve of mercenary marriages

Lady Bracknell moves RC

                  When I wed Lord Bracknell I had no fortune (*pause*) of any
                  kind,

But I never allowed it to dwell on my mind.

Algernon takes Cecily and moves down to Lady Bracknell

Algernon (*speaking*) Aunt Augusta, will you please give me your permission to marry the sweetest, dearest, prettiest girl in the whole world?

Lady Bracknell (*singing*) My child, your engagement will be
Approved by me most assuredly.
Dear boy, you can both proceed
Now your uncle and I have agreed.

(*Speaking*) Cecily.
Cecily Yes, Lady Bracknell?
Lady Bracknell You may kiss me!

Cecily kisses Lady Bracknell as Algernon backs away to the table LC

And Cecily.
Cecily Yes, Lady Bracknell?
Lady Bracknell In future you will address me as Aunt Augusta.
Cecily Thank you, Aunt Augusta.

Lady Bracknell sits in the settee beside Gwendolen and Cecily moves to Algernon by the chair US *of the table*

Lady Bracknell The marriage, I think, had better take place quite soon. I am not in favour of long engagements. They give people the opportunity of finding out each other's character before marriage, which is never advisable.

Jack (*moving into* C) I beg your pardon for interrupting you, Lady Bracknell, but this engagement is quite out of the question. I am Miss Cardew's guardian and she cannot marry without my consent until she comes of age. That consent I absolutely decline to give.

Lady Bracknell On what grounds may I ask? Algernon is an extremely, I would say ostentatiously, eligible young man. He has nothing, but he looks everything. What more can one desire?

Jack It pains me very much to have to speak frankly to you, Lady Bracknell, about your nephew, but the fact is that I do not approve of his moral character. I suspect him of being untruthful.

Algernon and Cecily look at him in indignant amazement

Lady Bracknell Untruthful! My nephew Algernon? Impossible! He had a university education.

Jack I fear there can be no possible doubt about the matter. This afternoon during my temporary absence in London on an important question of romance, he obtained admission to my house by pretending to be my brother. (*He crosses to Algernon*) He then drank an entire pint bottle of my best champagne. (*He moves back to* C) Continuing his disgraceful deception he succeeded in the course of the afternoon in alienating the affections of my ward. (*He moves to Algernon*) What makes his conduct all the more heartless is that he was perfectly well aware from the first that

I have no brother, that I never had a brother, and that I don't intend to have a brother, not even of any kind.

Lady Bracknell Ahem! Mr Worthing, after careful consideration I have decided entirely to overlook my nephew's conduct to you.

Jack That is very generous of you, Lady Bracknell. My own decision, however, is unalterable. I decline to give my consent. (*He crosses below Algernon and Cecily to their* L)

Lady Bracknell (*to Cecily*) How old are you, sweet child?

Cecily (*moving into* C) Well, I am really only eighteen, but I always admit to twenty when I go to evening parties.

Lady Bracknell You are perfectly right to make some slight alteration. Indeed, no woman should ever be quite accurate about her age ... (*In a meditative manner*) Eighteen, but admitting to twenty at evening parties. Well, it will not be very long before you are of age and free from the restraint of tutelage. So I don't think your guardian's consent is, after all, a matter of any importance.

Jack moves to C, *as Cecily returns to Algernon*

Jack Pray excuse me, Lady Bracknell, for interrupting you again, but it is only fair to tell you that according to the terms of her grandfather's will, Miss Cardew does not come legally of age till she is thirty-five.

Lady Bracknell That does not seem to me to be a grave objection. Thirty-five is a very attractive age. London society is full of women of the very highest birth who have, of their own free choice, remained thirty-five for years. I see no reason why Cecily should not be even still more attractive at the age you mention than she is at present. And there will be a large accumulation of property.

Cecily (*going to him*) Algy, could you wait for me till I was thirty-five?

Algernon Of course I could, Cecily. You know I could.

Cecily Yes, I felt it instinctively, but I couldn't wait all that time. I hate waiting even five minutes for anybody.

Algernon Then what is to be done, Cecily?

Cecily I don't know, Mr Moncrieff. (*She moves to* DLC *below Algernon*)

Lady Bracknell My dear Mr Worthing, as Miss Cardew states positively that she cannot wait till she is thirty-five—a remark which I am bound to say seems to me to show a somewhat impatient nature—I would beg of you to reconsider your decision.

Jack But my dear Lady Bracknell, the matter is entirely in your own hands. The moment you consent to my marriage with Gwendolen, I will most gladly allow your nephew to form an alliance with my ward.

Lady Bracknell (*rising*) You must be quite aware that what you propose is out of the question.

Jack Then a passionate celibacy is all that any of us can look forward to.

Lady Bracknell That is not the destiny I propose for Gwendolen. Algernon, of course, can choose for himself. (*She pulls out her watch*) Come, my dear, we have already missed five, if not six trains.

Gwendolen rises and moves towards Jack

To miss any more might expose us to comment on the platform.

Dr Chasuble enters dressed in vestments and comes to the R of Jack and Algernon

Dr Chasuble Everything is quite ready for the christenings, gentlemen.

Lady Bracknell The christenings, sir! Is not that somewhat premature?

Dr Chasuble (*looking rather puzzled, and pointing to Jack and Algernon*) Both these gentlemen have expressed a desire for immediate baptism.

Lady Bracknell At their age? The idea is grotesque and irreligious. Algernon, I forbid you to be baptized. I will not hear of such excesses.

Dr Chasuble Am I to understand then that there are to be no christenings at all this afternoon?

Jack I don't think that, as things are now, it would be of much practical value to either of us, Dr Chasuble.

Dr Chasuble I am grieved to hear such sentiments from you, Mr Worthing. They savour of the heretical views of the Anabaptists, views that I have completely refuted in four of my unpublished sermons. However, as your present mood seems to be peculiarly secular, I will return to the church at once as Miss Prism has been waiting for me in the vestry for over an hour and a half.

Lady Bracknell (*starting*) Miss Prism! Did I hear you mention a Miss Prism?

Dr Chasuble I am on my way to join her now.

Lady Bracknell (*anxiously*) One moment, sir. Is this Miss Prism a female of repellent aspect, remotely connected with education?

Dr Chasuble (*somewhat indignantly*) She is the most cultivated of ladies, and the very picture of respectability.

Lady Bracknell (*thoughtfully*) It is obviously the same person. I must see her at once. Let her be sent for. (*She sits again on the settee*)

Miss Prism enters hurriedly and moves to Dr Chasuble L

Miss Prism I was told you expected me in the vestry, dear Canon. I have been waiting there for almost an hour and a half.

Miss Prism catches sight of Lady Bracknell who fixes her with a stony glare. Miss Prism grows pale and quails looking round for a means of escape

Lady Bracknell (*in a severe, judicial voice*) Come here, Prism!

Miss Prism bows her head in shame and moves DS

Prism! Where is that baby?

Lady Bracknell rises and follows Miss Prism. There is general consternation. Miss Prism makes no answer

The Lights change to give the room a more court-like appearance and all the Servants crowd into the room

Twenty-eight years ago, Prism, you left Lord Bracknell's house, number one hundred and four Upper Grosvenor Street, in charge of a perambulator that contained a baby of the male sex. You never returned. A few weeks later when the perambulator was found it only contained the manuscript of a three-volume novel of more than usually revolting sentimentality.

Miss Prism starts in involuntary indignation

But the baby was not there! Prism! Where is that baby?

Everyone looks at Miss Prism

Music No. 21: Borne in a Handbag

Miss Prism (*speaking*) I admit with shame that I do not know—I only wish I did.

Lady Bracknell, Jack, Gwendolen, Algernon, Cecily and Dr Chasuble all come in closer behind Miss Prism. The Servants stand in groups US. *Miss Prism has* DSC *to herself. She tries hard to remember*

  (Singing)   I do recall that morning long ago
                  I planned a simple walk down Rotten Row.
                  As I gathered my things together in the hall,
                  I carefully wrapped the baby in his shawl.

Everyone confides or agrees with the people next to them as they repeat the last line of each verse

All   She carefully wrapped the baby in his shawl.
Miss Prism (*suddenly nursing a secret rapture*)
                  For years I nursed a very big desire
                  To write a novel full of love and fire.
                  Oh, picture my joy when I wrote the final word
                  The night before this terrible thing occurred,
All   The night before this terrible thing occurred.

Miss Prism appeals out front as Cecily and Algernon move behind her to further LC

Miss Prism   How can we know in times of great abstraction
                  It might affect our every single action?
                  Instead of placing the baby in his basinette
                  I must have wrapped the clothes around my novelette.
All   She must have wrapped the clothes around her novelette.

Miss Prism (*appealing to everyone*)
                  How many things in our life would we change
                  If only fate would let us rearrange
                  Some of the secret moments from our past
                  Then our souls would find true peace at last.

Miss Prism turns tearfully US

Lady Bracknell (*impatiently; speaking*) But what did you do with the baby, Prism?

Miss Prism (*facing the front again; singing*)
        I've tried so hard to recall what happened next
        But all I do is end up quite perplexed.
        (*Staring into space*)
        The only thing I see is my leather bag,
        I must have placed the baby in that handbag.
All   She must have placed the baby in her handbag.

Lady Bracknell who is moving away R *turns startled when she hears the word handbag*

Lady Bracknell A handbag! (*She sits on the settee*)
Miss Prism (*gazing into the distance*)
        I can't say now what path or road I took

She puts her hand on her head

        My thoughts were on the future of my book
        And believing that it held my own creation
        I left the handbag in a railway station.
All   She left the handbag in a railway station.

Jack moves down to Miss Prism L

Jack (*speaking*) What was the name of the station?
Miss Prism (*with another change of mood*)
        The name was there on every single wall;
        (*happily praising the Queen*)
        She is the greatest monarch of them all.
Jack (*speaking*) Victoria! I knew it! Quick, tell me the line.
Miss Prism (*coming down to earth*)
        A notice said it was the Brighton Line.
All   A notice said it was the Brighton Line.

   Jack exits hurriedly

Miss Prism   How many things in our life would we change
        If only fate would let us rearrange
        Some of the secret moments from the past
        Then our souls would find true peace at last.

   Jack enters carrying a large leather handbag. He hurries down to Miss Prism L *and pushes the bag into her hands*

Jack Is this the handbag?

Miss Prism examines it for a moment — then a look of recognition comes into her eyes

Miss Prism
   (*singing*)   That scratch was made by the side of an omnibus

She finds a stain which embarrasses her

        And the alcohol stain that caused a little fuss.

(*Looking at the top*)
And my initials stamped in bronze by Stone and Raby.
(*Quite firmly*)
This handbag is the one that held the baby.

Jack shows the handbag to Algernon who takes it

All   This handbag is the one that held the baby.

Jack moves to Miss Prism and speaks in a pathetic voice

Jack Miss Prism, more is restored to you than your handbag. I was the baby you placed in it.
Miss Prism (*amazed*) You?
Jack (*embracing her*) Yes . . . Mother!
Miss Prism (*recoiling in indignant astonishment*) Mr Worthing! I am unmarried.
Jack Unmarried! That is a serious blow.

Jack recovers and moves to Lady Bracknell, appeals to her, moving on to Gwendolen, then to Algernon and finally back to Miss Prism

(*To Lady Bracknell*) But who has the right to cast a stone against one who has suffered? (*To Gwendolen*) Cannot repentance wipe out one act of folly? (*To Algernon*) Why should there be one law for men, and another for women? (*Returning to Miss Prism*) Mother, I forgive you. (*He tries to embrace her again*)
Miss Prism (*still more indignantly*) Mr Worthing, there is some error. (*She points to Lady Bracknell*) There is the lady who can tell you who you really are.

Miss Prism backs away US, *leaving Jack* DS

Jack (*after a pause and moving* C) Lady Bracknell, I hate to seem inquisitive, but would you kindly inform me who I am?
Lady Bracknell (*rising*)
                           The truth gave me a moment of disbelief.
                           You are the son of my sister, Jane Moncrieff,
                           So I'm pleased to tell you Prism's not your mother,
                           You are in fact Algernon's brother!
All   Algernon's brother?

The room lighting returns to normal and all the Servants exit

Jack crosses to Algernon and Cecily

Jack Algy's brother! Then I have a brother after all. I knew I had a brother! I always said I had a brother! Cecily—how could you have ever doubted that I had a brother? (*He takes hold of Algernon and drags him to be introduced to Dr Chasuble, Miss Prism and Gwendolen*) Dr Chasuble, my unfortunate brother. Miss Prism, my unfortunate brother. Gwendolen, my unfortunate brother. (*He takes Algernon back towards the table* L) Algy, you young scoundrel, you will have to treat me with more respect in the future. You have never behaved to me like a brother in all your life.

Algernon Well, not till today, old boy, I admit. I did my best, however, though I was a bit out of practice. (*He shakes hands with Jack*)

Gwendolen (*crossing to Jack*) My own! But what own are you? What is your Christian name, now that you have become someone else?

Jack Good heavens . . . ! I had quite forgotten that point. Your decision on the subject of my name is final, I suppose?

Gwendolen I never change my mind.

Cecily What a noble nature you have, Gwendolen!

Jack Then the question had better be cleared up at once. (*He crosses to Lady Bracknell*) Lady Bracknell, a moment. At the time when Miss Prism left me in the handbag, had I been christened already?

Lady Bracknell Every luxury that money could buy, including christening, had been lavished on you by your fond and doting parents.

Jack Then I was christened! That is settled. Now, what name was I given? Let me know the worst.

Lady Bracknell Being the eldest son, you were naturally christened after your father.

Jack (*irritably*) Yes, but what was my father's Christian name?

Lady Bracknell (*meditatively*) I cannot at the present moment recall what the general's Christian name was. But I have no doubt he had one.

Jack Algy! Can't you recollect what our father's Christian name was?

Algernon My dear boy, we were never even on speaking terms. He died before I was a year old.

Jack His name would appear in the Army lists of the period, I suppose, Lady Bracknell?

Lady Bracknell The general was essentially a man of peace, except in his domestic life. But I have no doubt his name would appear in any military directory.

Jack The Army lists of the last forty years are here. Merriman, get me "Generals".

Merriman hurries to the bookcase, extracts a volume and hands it to Jack who impatiently turns the pages

These delightful records should have been my constant study.

Jack paces DS with the book, followed by Miss Prism and Gwendolen at his sides and Dr Chasuble, Algernon and Cecily behind

M. Generals . . . Mallam, Maxbohm, Magley, what ghastly names they have—Markby, Migsby, Mobbs, Moncrieff! Lieutenant eighteen forty, Captain, Lieutenant-Colonel, Colonel, General eighteen sixty-nine. Christian names—(*he pauses and says quietly*)—Ernest John.

Jack hands the book to Gwendolen who with Miss Prism at her R and Algernon and Cecily at her L examines it

I always told you, Gwendolen, my name was Ernest, didn't I? Well, it is Ernest after all.

Merriman, knowing his master's taste and sensing an impending celebration, exits to prepare champagne

Lady Bracknell (*rising*) Yes, I remember now that the general was called Ernest. I knew I had some particular reason for disliking the name.

Gwendolen hands the book to Dr Chasuble who moves RC followed by Miss Prism while Cecily and Algernon break to LC

Gwendolen Ernest! My own Ernest! I felt from the first that you could have no other name!

Jack meets Gwendolen C

Jack Gwendolen, it is a terrible thing for a man to find out suddenly that all his life he's been speaking nothing but the truth. Can you forgive me?
Gwendolen I can.
Jack My own one!
Dr Chasuble (*to Miss Prism*) Laetitia! (*He embraces her*)
Miss Prism (*enthusiastically*) Frederick! At last (*She kisses Dr Chasuble*)
Algernon Cecily! At last! (*He embraces her*)

Music No. 22: One Love/The Importance of Being Earnest

Jack and Gwendolen, Algernon and Cecily, Miss Prism and Dr Chasuble waltz in a celebration dance as everyone except Lady Bracknell sings

All   One love here in my heart,
                 One dream when we're apart.
                 Oh I need you, adore you, I love you.
                 Darling, please say you'll be mine.
                 Darling, please tell me you're mine.

                 Give me your hand, sweet valentine.
                 Give me your lips red as the wine.
                 Say that you love me, set my heart free,
                 Tell me you'll share your whole life with me.

Jack (*speaking*) Merriman! Champagne for everyone!

Merriman and Servants enter with trays of champagne glasses

Jack, Gwendolen, Cecily, Algernon, Miss Prism, and Dr Chasuble all toast each other

The Servants remove furniture for the final bows

Lady Bracknell who, up to now, has been an onlooker, comes down between Jack and Gwendolen who are C

Lady Bracknell (*interrupting the music and general hubbub with obvious disapproval*) My nephew, you seem to be displaying signs of triviality.
Jack On the contrary, Aunt Augusta. I've now realized for the first time the vital importance of being Ernest. (*He takes Gwendolen DS*)

Gwendolen   The importance of being Ernest
(*singing*)   Is something I'm certain about.
                  Your name is divine

And it goes well with mine,
It sounds so honest and free.
I'll never discover
True love with another
I've made up my mind you see.

All line up to sing the last verse

All   The importance of being Ernest
Is something that will never change.
The fates have decreed
And their hearts have agreed
No-one but Ernest will do.
So kindly remember
They'll never surrender
To anyone else but you.

Music No. 23: Curtain Calls

Music No. 24: Play-out

CURTAIN

FURNITURE AND PROPERTY LIST

ACT I

SCENE 1

On stage: Park bench

Off stage: Basket with posies and buttonholes **(Flower Girl)**
Victorian pram with bedding and baby **(Nursemaid)**—*required twice*

Personal: **3 Young Men, Mr Lake, Father:** walking sticks
2 Mothers, 3 Daughters: parasols
Algernon: fob watch

SCENE 2

On stage: Shop truck. *On it:* bolts of cloth, hats, hat boxes
Dummy LC with Norfolk jacket
Dummy RC with loose cover
Curtain across changing alcove
Hat/cane stand. *In it:* 4 walking sticks
Table. *On it:* velvet cloth, assorted hats (Victorian), magazines, swatch
book, clothes brush, ashtray
2 chairs
Shop bell
Trousers
Cheval mirror

Off stage: **Jack**'s jacket **(Assistant)**
Jack's hat and cane **(2 Assistants)**
Pile of folded shirts **(Assistant)**
Algernon's smoking jacket **(Lane)**

Personal: **Algernon:** walking stick, gloves, cigarette case

SCENE 3

On stage: Bookshelf with books and copy of the *Railway Guide*
2 large pot plants
Table. *On it:* large silver tray with pink china set of 4 cups, 4 saucers, 4 side
plates, milk-jug, sugar-bowl, 4 cloth doilies, plate of bread and butter,
small vase of flowers

2 chairs
Settee. *On it:* cushions
Plate with 2 small cucumber sandwiches for **Algernon**
Servants' bell on wall US

Off stage: Pot of tea **(Lane)**
Day jacket, hat, gloves, cane **(Maids)**

Personal: **Lady Bracknell:** parasol, handbag containing notebook and pencil
Gwendolen: notebook, pencil
Algernon: notebook, pencil

SCENE 4

On stage: Garden table. *On it:* books including German Grammar, Political Econ-
omy, Geography, diary, pencils, **Miss Prism's** parasol
2 chairs
Hammock chair
Wicker table. *On it:* books
Garden bench
Rustic arch with trailing pink roses
Props for **Servants:** trident **(Britannia)**, scroll **(Disraeli)**, mace **(John Bull)**,
lantern **(Florence Nightingale)**, telescope **(Nelson)**, orb and sceptre
(Queen Victoria)

Off stage: Silver salver with calling card **(Merriman)**

Personal: **Cecily:** ring, watch, bangle, brooch *(required throughout)*

SCENE 5

On stage: Flower bed with selection of flowers including red roses
Sundial

Off stage: Parasol **(Miss Prism)**

SCENE 6

On stage: Garden table
2 chairs
Garden bench

Off stage: Box of letters tied up with blue ribbon, diary, pencil **(Cecily)**
2 large suitcases, 2 medium suitcases, small lunch case, 2 small hat boxes,
gold-topped cane, Gladstone bag **(Servants)**

Personal: **Jack:** black-bordered handkerchief

ACT II

SCENE 1

On stage: 2 garden benches. *On R one:* 2 swords in sheaths. *On L one:* **Cecily's** diary
and pencil
Seat for **Queen Victoria**
Props for **Servants:** telescope **(Nelson)**, lantern, small Union Jack **(Florence Nightingale)**, trident **(Britannia)**, scroll, small Union Jack

(Disraeli), mace, small Union Jack **(John Bull)**, orb and sceptre **(Queen Victoria)**
2 large swagged Union Jack and Empire flags for **Merriman** and **Servant**
Small Union Jacks for **Maids**

Off stage: 2 tea trolleys—see below **(Servants)**

Personal: **Gwendolen:** *lorgnette*, diary

SCENE 2

On stage: As Scene 1, plus:
Garden benches set further L and R
2 tea trolleys. *On them:* white tablecloth, lace overlay, milk-jug, sugar-bowl, tea-strainer, sugar-tongs, plates, 2 cups, 2 saucers, 2 teaspoons, 2 knives, 2 cake forks, plate of bread and butter, plate of muffins, pot of jam, pot of honey, cake on cake stand with cake knife, 2 pots of tea, tray with mat

Off stage: Table **(Servants)**
2 chairs **(Servants)**
Vase of flowers **(Maid)**

SCENE 3

On stage: 2 garden benches
Conservatory truck. *On it:* 2 large pot plants, 4 small potted flowers

SCENE 4

On stage: Conservatory truck
Settee
Table
2 chairs
Bookshelves. *On them:* leather-bound books including *Army Lists*

Off stage: Large leather handbag **(Jack)**
Trays of champagne glasses **(Servants)**

Personal: **Lady Bracknell:** watch, *lorgnette*

ACT ONE : Scene 1   GREEN PARK

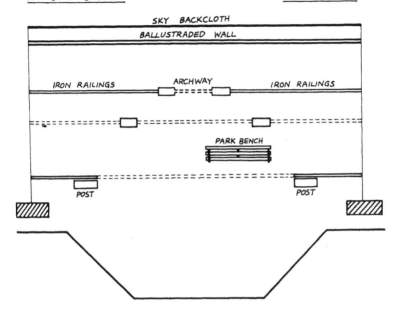

ACT ONE: Scene 2   LAKE'S OUTFITTERS

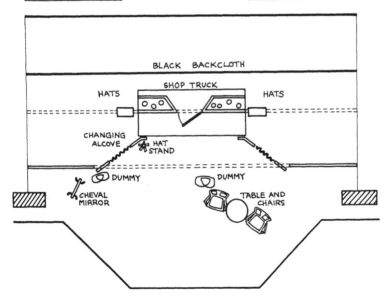

ACT ONE : Scene 3   ALGERNON'S FLAT

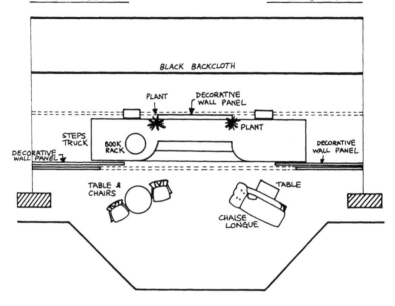

ACT ONE : Scene 4   GROUNDS OF MANOR HOUSE

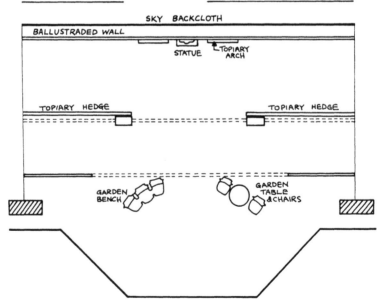

ACT ONE : Scene 5   <u>SECLUDED GARDEN</u>

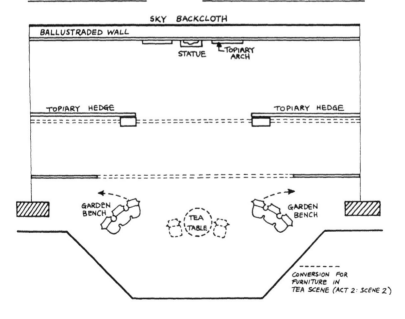

SKY BACKCLOTH
BALLUSTRADED WALL
STATUE

TOPIARY HEDGE   TOPIARY ARCH   TOPIARY HEDGE

ARBOUR BUSHES   ARBOUR BUSHES

CONIFER   CONIFER

SUN DIAL
AND
FLOWER BED

ACT TWO : Scene 1 & 2   TOPIARY GARDEN & TERRACE

SKY BACKCLOTH
BALLUSTRADED WALL
STATUE   TOPIARY ARCH

TOPIARY HEDGE   TOPIARY HEDGE

GARDEN BENCH   TEA TABLE   GARDEN BENCH

CONVERSION FOR
FURNITURE IN
TEA SCENE (ACT 2: SCENE 2)

ACT TWO: Scene 3   CONSERVATORY

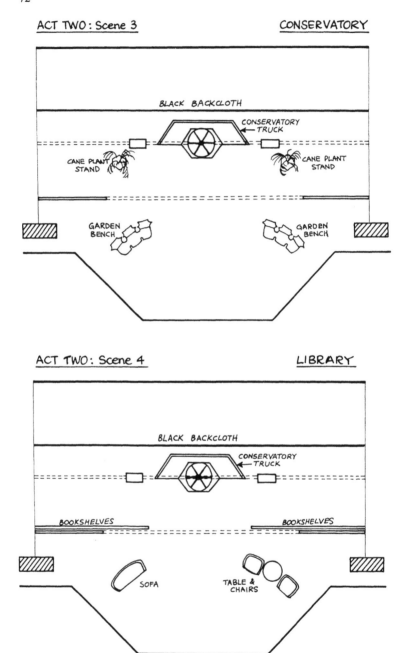

BLACK BACKCLOTH

CONSERVATORY TRUCK

CANE PLANT STAND

CANE PLANT STAND

GARDEN BENCH

GARDEN BENCH

ACT TWO: Scene 4   LIBRARY

BLACK BACKCLOTH

CONSERVATORY TRUCK

BOOKSHELVES

BOOKSHELVES

SOFA

TABLE & CHAIRS

ACT ONE: Scene 6   THE TRELLIS GARDEN

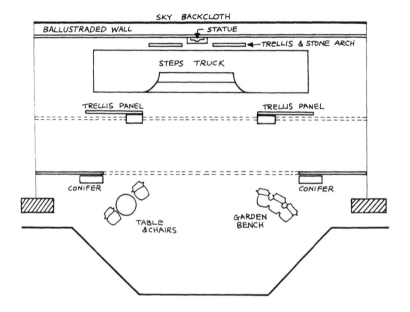

LIGHTING PLOT

Property fittings required: *nil*

Various simple interior and exterior settings

ACT I

To open: General exterior lighting

Cue 1	**Father** leads **Daughter** and others off *Fade lights* US	(Page 2)
Cue 2	**Algernon** enters and moves LC *Spot follows him—cut as he exits*	(Page 2)
Cue 3	When ready for Scene 2 *Bring up general interior lighting*	(Page 2)
Cue 4	**Algernon** moves downstage *Fade lights* US	(Page 8)
Cue 5	When ready for Scene 3 *Bring up general interior lighting*	(Page 8)
Cue 6	**Algernon** (*singing*): "... a gentleman can find ..." *Fade lights* US	(Page 20)
Cue 7	When ready for Scene 4 *Bring up general exterior sunny lighting*	(Page 20)
Cue 8	**Cecily** exits running into the house *Fade lights*	(Page 27)
Cue 9	When ready for Scene 5 *Bring up general exterior lighting*	(Page 27)
Cue 10	**Miss Prism** and **Dr Chasuble** exit *Fade lights*	(Page 29)
Cue 11	When ready for Scene 6 *Bring up general exterior lighting*	(Page 30)
Cue 12	**Jack** pulls off **Algernon** with him *Fade to Black-out*	(Page 38)

ACT II

To open: General exterior lighting

Cue 13	As Scene 3 opens *Change to light and airy lighting on conservatory*	(Page 51)

EFFECTS PLOT

ACT I

Cue 1   **Jack** sits on the settee   (Page 9)
            Doorbell rings

ACT II

No cues

MADE AND PRINTED IN GREAT BRITAIN BY
LATIMER TREND & COMPANY LTD PLYMOUTH

MADE IN ENGLAND

Lightning Source UK Ltd.
Milton Keynes UK
UKHW010700140219
337286UK00006B/79/P